THE
RESET
BOOK

HOW TO BOUNCE BACK FROM A CRISIS

MAGNUS LINDKVIST

FOR OTHER TITLES
IN THE SERIES...

CONCISE
ADVICE
LAB

SMALL BOOKS: BIG IDEAS

CLEVER CONTENT, DYNAMIC IDEAS, PRACTICAL
SOLUTIONS AND ENGAGING VISUALS –
A CATALYST TO INSPIRE NEW WAYS OF THINKING
AND PROBLEM-SOLVING IN A COMPLEX WORLD

lidpublishing.com/books/concise-advice

To my father, Bo, the bounceback artist
(1948–2022)

Published by
LID Publishing
An imprint of LID Business Media Ltd.
LABS House, 15-19 Bloomsbury Way,
London, WC1A 2TH, UK

info@lidpublishing.com
www.lidpublishing.com

A member of:

businesspublishersroundtable.com

Printed by Severn, Gloucester

ISBN: 978-1-911687-68-9
ISBN: 978-1-911687-69-6 (ebook)

Cover and page design: Caroline Li

THE RESET BOOK

HOW TO BOUNCE BACK FROM A CRISIS

MAGNUS LINDKVIST

MADRID | MEXICO CITY | LONDON
BUENOS AIRES | BOGOTA | SHANGHAI

CONTENTS

INTRODUCTION
THE ART OF RESETTING

We predicted that we would have flying cars by the year 2020.

We got face masks and lockdowns instead.

A crisis happens when our expectations collide with reality in a way that leaves us whiplashed. It lies at the intersection of expectations and reality.

The future is a grand illusion where all our wildest dreams and nightmares come true.

The present just kind of stumbles along with all its faults and short-comings. We run errands, (fail to) complete tasks, worry about stuff, and daydream about lost love and lost horizons.

The past is something a lucky few can blank out completely. For the rest of us, it's an anchor holding us back, a story leading us astray, or a path that would have gone a different direction if only we had gone left or right at some crucial fork in the road.

As humans, we are stuck at an intersection called the present, haunted by days gone by and with an unreliable, slightly delusional guide to tomorrow.

"

There will come a time when you believe everything is finished. That will be the beginning.

"

Louis L'Amour,
Lonely On The Mountain

The words 'good luck!' come to mind.

For over two decades, I made a living by studying, writing and speaking about the future.

In February 2020, I told hotel owners from around the world that the future was bright. This was just after I had been a keynote speaker at an office supply company and just before I went off to address an audience of concert promotors from across Europe and the United States. My message to them was that the future was full of promise and opportunity.

About a month later, I was lying at home with nothing to do, all my speaking engagements cancelled, watching raindrops fall outside my window and economies crashing around the world on the news.

So much for my optimistic outlook.

I felt a sense of guilt and shame for having misled people with promises of greener pastures in the magical lands of tomorrow. Everything I had learned had been thrown out the window.

And my professional failure was only the beginning.

In the space of a few years, I lost my business, my marriage and my sense of self-worth. I grieved, and I felt sorry for myself.

I felt like life was unfair and became increasingly isolated and alone. I often hummed the lyrics to a forgotten rock song: "Everybody loves a winner, but when you lose, you lose alone."

Then something happened. In the summer of 2021, I became curious about what others had felt and done in my situation. I read novels and self-help books. I listened to relationship podcasts and watched documentaries. I spoke to people I met in bars, in airports and on Zoom. This opened my eyes to a new world, far from the keynote speeches I had, rather one-dimensionally, been delivering.

I found unexpected sources of wisdom in psychology, history, popular culture, science and business case studies. In this book, I have mixed these insights into a blender of ideas and hope they might help someone else through a crisis.

This book is not about all the ills that befall us in life.

It is a book about how you can get back on track when your personal life, your career and your world have been derailed.

The Reset Book is about what happens when the natural order of things is broken up and we are thrown out of our familiar realm into... well, we cannot be sure.

It is a book about the art of resetting, whether it's your love life after a broken heart, your business after bankruptcy, your artistic direction after the zeitgeist has shifted or your entire life's direction after some unexpected event takes you by surprise on some Tuesday morning.

The Reset Book will not bore you with new-age psychobabble. It will present findings based on real-world examples. Neither will *The Reset Book* propose some devious seven-step model where all the steps strangely begin with the same letter. Instead, you will get a plethora of different insights with the hope that you will be able to jump around to sections that suit your particular situation or need.

The Reset Book does not promise some eternal purpose or a happily-ever-after ending. There are many 'secret recipes to happiness' books and blog posts that all fail to consider the short half-life of feelings or that emotional experiences are too subjective to force into a universal mould.

The Reset Book will not dwell on the pain and scars that life inevitably leaves in us and on us. Losing a job, a marriage or a loved one is painful, and, if you are still suffering, psychological counselling might be a better use of your time than this book.

The purpose of this book is not to nourish grievances or console you in your darkest hour; it is to help you find a path towards fresh thinking about your life, your business and the world at large. It is a book for those who have lost their way and want to find it again.

Let the journey begin!

THE GROUNDHOG WAY
HOW THIS BOOK IS ORGANIZED

The movie *Groundhog Day* serves as a perfect blueprint to use when navigating a crisis.

When the self-centred weatherman Phil, played by Bill Murray, finds himself stuck in a time loop and forced to live the same day repeatedly in the small town of Punxsutawney, Pennsylvania, he goes through five distinct phases.

First, he is in denial. Time loops are not something you stumble upon daily. If this were to happen to you, you would probably suspect that you were dreaming or that somebody had snuck a powerful hallucinogenic drug into your morning coffee.

Then, Phil becomes angry. It is unfair that he has got stuck in a time loop in the middle of nowhere for no reason. He takes out his anger on other people and himself.

This is followed by a third phase, where Phil starts to experiment with all the possibilities a life with no morning-after consequences entails, from casual sex to pure narcissism.

This is where he hits a low point. Phil repeatedly tries to kill himself but wakes up every morning in the same bed to the tune of "I Got You Babe" by Sonny and Cher.

Finally, in the movie's last act, Phil decides to use the time loop to better himself, learn new skills and work slowly towards more altruistic goals. When he reaches these goals, the time loop vanishes as mysteriously as it first appeared. Phil wakes up to a new morning, a changed man.

One of the movie's screenwriters, Danny Rubin, was influenced by a clinical study outlining the five stages of grief: denial, anger, bargaining, depression and acceptance. Although the model has been criticized by doctors and trauma survivors for being too simplistic and not universally applicable, it can help us to understand, on a broad level, how we humans process new situations sequentially.

Take the Covid-19 pandemic as viewed through social media posts as an example.

The World Health Organization infamously tweeted on 14 January 2020 that "preliminary investigations conducted by the Chinese authorities have found no clear evidence of human-to-human transmission of the novel coronavirus." Contrary to the assertions of conspiracy theorists, the tweet did not stem from malevolence or a desire to mislead but from the available data at the time. However, it created a false sense of security and put the world in a state of denial.

As countries closed down in early spring, an outpouring of anger followed. Politicians were forced to make swift decisions about how best to cope with the virus, and an abundance of contradictory information made it difficult to draw simple conclusions. News relies on velocity. Facts require slow, deliberate thinking.

"

A book must be the axe for the frozen sea within us.

"

Franz Kafka

After the first wave had come and gone, societies bargained and debated about what approach to take if and when the virus struck again. Which it did. And this time, there was a deluge of negative emotions proclaiming the death of everything – freedom and democracy, even civilization itself. There was also the sorrow of lives lost.

Some people are still deeply embedded in one or many of these stages. Others have moved on to a phase of acceptance, albeit quietly and reluctantly.

We will doubtlessly debate and study these remarkable years for decades to come. However, for now, they serve as an example of how humans deal with events in a sequential, if not always orderly, way.

Groundhog Day serves as a loose basis for how this book is organized.

Firstly, we will examine how denial and other mental traps are the first defence when stuff – or the other s-word – happens.

Secondly, we will look at the emotional response that events big and small tend to trigger in us and what to do about it.

Thirdly, we will look at how change enables us to see the world anew.

Finally, we will look at how resetting emotions, resources and rules enables us to live with new direction – forever changed but not necessarily happy ever after.

Knowledge grows exponentially, not linearly, rendering our brains hopeless in our attempts to predict the future based on the past.

Neil deGrasse Tyson

PART ONE

DENIAL

CHAPTER 1
DELIGHTFUL
DELUSIONS

Crises begin by wasting time. They not only start but are also aggravated by the fact that we deny what we are seeing in front of us.

In the early 1990s, the world's largest record store was Tower Records, which had outlets on three continents and earned hundreds of millions of dollars in revenue from selling music packaged as compact discs, vinyl records and cassette tapes. The founder, Russell Solomon, was asked whether the company feared digital downloads or, as the question was phrased, "beaming music into people's homes." Solomon answered that beaming technology might come along someday, but it would happen over a long period, enabling Tower Records to gradually change its focus and deal with the situation.

Solomon, along with other human beings, did not have the gift of foresight, so when he predicted the pace of technological development, he really had no idea what the reality would be. He was telling a story to make himself and his company feel good. Leadership is the ability to tell a compelling story so that other people will follow you.

But this particular story turned out wrong, and Tower Records filed for bankruptcy in the early 2000s.

"

As powerful as the desire to deny atrocities is the conviction that denial does not work.

Judith Lewis Herman

Telling misleading stories about the future is the first stage of denial.

A graver example of this is Nobel Peace Prize winner Norman Angell, whose book *The Great Illusion* persuasively argued that "the economic cost of the war was so great that no one could hope to gain by starting a war the consequences of which would be so disastrous." In other words, a European war was improbable.

The book was published just before the First World War broke out.

Like the rest of us, Tower Records executives and Nobel Prize-winning authors are storytelling creatures. We want to fit the chaotic stream of actions, impressions and events that we face daily into a neat narrative. In doing this, we simplify, reduce and streamline. A natural consequence is that we emphasize and focus on some parts, and we disregard and deny others.

Denial is one of civilization's most potent forces and a vital ingredient in us functioning properly as human beings. If we were to consider and calculate every single risk we faced daily – from slipping in the shower to being hit by a runaway car – we would never get out of bed.

If we never risked losing money or having our hearts broken, we would never take our chances on the stock- or dating market. Life is not one giant leap of faith but myriad small skips and jumps over puddles of possibilities.

This is enabled by a deceptive machine sitting right above the shoulders of all human beings. We would never accept other bodily organs being as flawed as the brain. Here is just a short list of some of its shortcomings:

- **Availability bias**: thinking that examples of things that come readily to mind are more representative than is the case
- **Hindsight bias**: also known as the knew-it-all-along phenomenon, this is the tendency for people to perceive past events as having been more predictable than they were
- **Confirmation bias**: the tendency to search for, interpret, favour and recall information in a way that confirms or supports one's prior beliefs or values
- **Optimism bias**: the tendency to believe that we are less likely than others to experience an adverse event
- **Normalcy bias**: the tendency for people to believe that things in life will continue to go the way they always have

To these add conjunction fallacies, induction errors, contamination effects, affect heuristics, scope neglect, overconfidence in calibration and bystander apathy, and also take into consideration that this is a list of things that affect a fully functional adult brain.

When your knee joint or heart valve does something wrong, you feel pain or discomfort and go to see a doctor. However, you feel nothing when your brain falls into any of these traps. You might even feel good.

Take the conspiracy theory known as the Great Reset[1] as an example.

The Great Reset began as a conference theme for the World Economic Forum but was highjacked by outsiders and remodeled as a sinister scheme entailing the usual suspects of secretive societies in bed with political leaders wreaking havoc on the oblivious masses for the sake of money, power and the blood of innocent babies. A simple web search will suffice if you want to know more. Just be careful not to find contradictory evidence lest your conspiracy bubble pops.

Conspiracy theories are not uncommon, especially in societies characterized by low trust in institutions. They capitalize on the human need for order, solutions and direction, no matter how misleading. They usually contain grains of truth interspersed with random speculation, pure fantasy and malevolent interpretation. The core purpose of a conspiracy theory is to make its followers feel a sense of community and belonging. We – the enlightened – have discovered something profound that you – sheepish followers – have not. It is a kind of feel-good tribe. If the human brain reacted to false information in the same way that our stomach reacts to spoiled meat, we would start vomiting every time somebody told us that the world is flat. In such circumstances, it is safe to assume that fewer people would subscribe to the 'flat-earth theory' – another conspiracy theory wherein people believe our planet is a disc, not a globe.

However, conspiracy theories are just an extreme manifestation of something we all do – tell stories that make us feel better about ourselves, the world and the future. Take the wedding oath that we will love someone in sickness and in health "till death us do part." Given divorce rates, this once sacred vow is best considered a feel-good ceremonial statement, not a legally binding, long-term promise.

Or take any New Year's resolution, for that matter. Most of us begin a new year with the idea of becoming a better person over the coming 12 months – somebody who reads or works out more, drinks less alcohol and is a better parent.

A month later, we are back to wine-drinking and general slacking.

The point here is not to berate us for being morally flawed individuals who lack willpower. It is to emphasize that stories are a vital part of our lives, no matter how blind they are to reality. A wedding ceremony with the words "I promise to love you forever unless we divorce, which has a 40-50% probability" would be more scientifically accurate but less romantic.

We live in delightful delusions.

Every crisis begins with denial.

1   This is probably a good time to point out that this book has nothing to do with the Great Reset apart from sharing the r-word, but thank you for buying my book anyway.

CHAPTER 2
OSTRICH MODE

Our attention functions like a radar. When awake, we are aware of our surroundings, but our attention zooms in on particular things – the food we eat, the phone in our hand, the players on the football pitch and so on. Outside this focus, things are constantly vying for our attention, but most of these attempts fail miserably, and we carry on eating, writing a text message or watching our team get clobbered by the opposite side.

Sometimes, however, something grabs our attention because it stands out from whatever is happening around us. It can be loud, colourful, beautiful, ugly or just downright strange. Like a blip on a radar screen, it tells us that this is worth our attention. We do not know what it is yet, but we should investigate. It all begins with a blip.

What does this have to do with going through a crisis and, more specifically, the denial phase? To answer, we should consider Neo, the reluctant hero played by Keanu Reeves in the 1999 science fiction masterpiece *The Matrix*. When we first see Neo, he is fast asleep in front of his computer, and we get the feeling that he spends too much time in that particular place. Suddenly the words "Wake up, Neo..." appear on the screen and, by coincidence, Neo awakes. He sits upright and takes off his earphones. Next the words "Matrix has you..." appear, to which Neo bewilderingly stammers, "What... what the hell?" He tries rebooting the computer, but nothing happens, and the words "Follow the white rabbit" appear instead. Two loud knocks on Neo's door follow, and the action begins.

In the theory of storytelling known as "The Hero's Journey," narrative arcs begin with a call to adventure. Luke Skywalker hearing about an imprisoned princess or Simba being banished from the Pride Lands into the desert by his evil uncle, Scar, are examples of a protagonist who leaves the comfort and status quo of the known world for the challenges and mysteries of the unknown world.

Similarly, when you go through a crisis, you are thrust from the ordinary life you lead into something strange and new. The portal comes in the shape of a blip or a glitch in the matrix.

Like Neo at the beginning of *The Matrix*, we float through parts of our life in a pleasantly self-delusional bubble. We tell ourselves that things are fine and the tasks around us matter, and we carry a feeling that this will somehow last forever, while knowing deep down that it is untrue.

When some small, unexpected thing comes along to pop the bubble, our instinct is usually to ignore it. The email you were not supposed to see was probably nothing. That slight discomfort in your lower back is not worth a doctor's visit. That brilliant idea that suddenly struck you in the shower slowly fades from your memory as you do nothing about it.

This is not because you are lazy, oblivious or ignorant. Or rather, it is not *only* because you are lazy, oblivious or ignorant. It is also because living life requires a sense of predictability and order to function. We can call this Ostrich Mode.

"

Our very eyes are sometimes like our judgments, blind.

"

William Shakespeare

Random experimentation with what you eat and whom you sleep with might be a good idea for a few years at university, but it would make life very difficult to navigate for your remaining decades. And, more importantly, random experimentation would become a boring, everyday routine. When a blip comes along, it is an inconvenience that we instinctively swat away like an irritating insect, often preferring comfort to the truth.

But Ostrich Mode can be dangerous. In a famous Swedish song about the sinking of the Titanic, the lyrics begin with the words "it started as a shiver on the lower decks, which filled us more with surprise than fear." Why would such a shiver alarm you if you had been told you were on an unsinkable ship?

Ostrich Mode can also be unprofitable. When Steve Ballmer, then CEO of Microsoft, was asked what he thought of the iPhone, which the company's rival Apple was about to launch, he famously laughed it off, believing it was too expensive and lacked a keyboard, which would, Ballmer scoffed, make it useless as a business tool.

Ballmer was hardly the first executive to misread the market. Laura Ashley, the fashion and interior decoration firm that was wildly successful in the 1980s, kept on selling floral dresses, curtains and blankets even when minimalism sailed up above the horizon in the early 1990s. Kodak kept making money from film stock when digital photography was taking over. Volkswagen kept making diesel engines, even tampering with the emissions software to correspond to new standards, while Tesla showed that the future was electric. In these cases, it is not enough to argue that the executives were stuck in Ostrich Mode. They were paid to generate

profits for their shareholders, and none of them was actively trying to sabotage their own business. The question, then, is why
intelligent, capable people keep doing the same thing when they
should be changing.

The answer has to do with poison.

CHAPTER 3
SUCCESS
IS TOXIC

When Nokia's chairman, Risto Siilasmaa, was asked why the once-dominant mobile phone manufacturer had nearly gone bankrupt, he answered that success is toxic. It can make an organization lazy, bureaucratic, entitled and paranoid. In the case of Nokia, too, Siilasmaa noticed a general lack of accountability – a sign that a company has grown far beyond its original dimensions. Success is something we strive towards as human beings. Whether in our personal or professional lives, like that elusive carrot dangling on a stick, success is best thought of as something that can spur us on and motivate us to improve, not an end goal in and of itself. To understand the toxicology of success, let us look at three wildly different examples taken from the diverse worlds of geopolitics, pop music stardom and household economics.

The first example begins with a famous book title. In the late 1980s, political scientist Francis Fukuyama wrote an article titled "The End of History?," which investigated whether history can be viewed as an evolutionary process and whether liberal democracy is the ultimate and final form of government for all nations. It was eloquent, curious and – as the question mark in the title suggests – an open, provocative question, not a fact. It came out just as the Cold War ended and the Soviet Union collapsed. It was republished as an entire book in 1992 with one significant difference in the title. The question mark had been dropped. This omission did not seem to matter in the coming decade as the world – led by the United States and Europe – enjoyed a phenomenally successful run economically, technologically and politically. It looked like every nation on earth would eventually become a miniature version of America or Sweden: democratic, prosperous and peaceful.

Wars, pandemics, terrorism and economic turmoil were relegated to past decades and centuries. We were now living in what was dubbed 'the New Economy.' The sense of success was so pervasive that few heeded the warnings about climate, radical terrorism or the possibility of viruses taking advantage of our global, interconnected system. The only risk was erroneously programmed computers wreaking havoc on New Year's Eve 1999 – the so-called Y2K problem – a prophecy that did not come to fruition and became something of a joke.

In hindsight, we were victims of our own success, believing that it would last forever and, more damagingly, that we were immune to the ills of history. We expected each other to be optimistic in life, society and business. Anything else was viewed with scorn and disdain.

Success is a blindfold.

The second example features George Michael, one of the most successful pop stars ever.

Born in London as Georgios Panayiotou, he was a shy boy with an English mother and a Greek father. He had a deep sense of guilt and shame about how he looked, his weight and his sexuality. With intense ambition, he rose to global fame, first with the duo Wham!

and later as a solo artist, producing number-one hits worldwide since the 1980s. But fame and success did not bring Michael happiness, and he infamously spent the later decades of his career in a downward spiral of drugs, arrests, lawsuits, car crashes and destructive relationships. He died a premature death at age 53.

It is common for wildly ambitious people to want to compensate for some inner shortcoming, and Michael is one of many who tried to mend a broken soul with money, rank and adulation. This can work for a little while since an outwardly-oriented person – writing songs, planning tours and performing on stage – has less mental space for painful introspection. But there comes a day when all external goals have been reached but the voices from within have not grown quiet. Money can buy many things but will not change your values or identity. Like a drug, success can work miracles in small doses but can be fatal when it takes over. Success should be a motivator, not a goal in itself.

The third and final example illustrates why success toxicology is relevant in a book about bouncing back after a crisis. It combines marital breakdowns with financial crashes.

In economics, there is something called the sunk cost fallacy – the phenomenon where a person is reluctant to abandon a strategy or course of action simply because they have invested heavily in it. Choosing to finish a boring movie at the cinema because you have paid for the ticket is an example of the sunk cost fallacy. Not divorcing someone just because you have been together for a long time is another example, as is holding on to a bad investment because selling it would become evidence of what a bad investment it had been.

"

Failure is hard, but success is far more dangerous. If you're successful at the wrong thing, the mix of praise and money and opportunity can lock you in forever.

"

Po Bronson

In other words, we stay the course when we should change it.

We do this because we tend to rationalize that something has value to us just because we have been doing it and believed in it for a long time, like a marriage or an investment strategy. When things change, we are reluctant to look at new evidence and count our losses, hoping that the greener pastures we once enjoyed might return. To sell off our assets or get a divorce would be to admit to ourselves and others that we had been wrong all along.

The success of what has been can stand in the way of what lies ahead. Like with Nokia, it can make us blind, lazy or disillusioned. The extent to which you fall under the spell of Ostrich Mode is a function of how successful you perceive your life to have been in the past.

CHAPTER 4
KANSAS MOMENTS

When journalist Kathryn Schulz's father died, she described the first phase as "those early, distorted days of mourning, when so much of the familiar world feels alien and inaccessible." Joan Didion, a novelist, called her memoir about the first year after her husband unexpectedly passed away *The Year of Magical Thinking*, alluding to the surreal nature of grief. In philosophy, that feeling is called 'solastalgia' and it describes the unease you feel when what you took to be the natural way of things – a father or wife living, for example – changes without your consent, and life does not feel as once it did.

When this happens, you are living in a 'Kansas Moment.'

According to researchers at the University of Turin, the movie most referenced by other movies is *The Wizard of Oz* (1939), near perfect example of good storytelling. And it isn't just movies – from Elton John's album *Goodbye Yellow Brick Road* to the musical *Wicked*, the story of Dorothy's accidental journey to the magical land of Oz has many symbolic references that are used to this day in all kinds of media: the man behind the curtain, "Ding-Dong! The Witch Is Dead!" and, of course, "We're not in Kansas anymore." These are the words Dorothy says to her dog, Toto, when they first land in the magical, Technicolor Munchkinland of Oz. We can refer to this as the original Kansas Moment – when an insight grips you that everything around you has changed, or is about to change, radically.

A Kansas Moment is the first step out of denial and into a new world.

The first step out of denial is a sense that something new and unreal is about to unfold.

When the first plane struck the World Trade Center on 11 September 2001, most people believed they had witnessed a tragic accident. When the second plane hit, we all went through a collective Kansas Moment of the darker kind.

Similarly, a lab result in a doctor's office or seeing your loved one in the arms of another will instantly switch your life's soundtrack from the major to the minor key.

But there are bright Kansas Moments too.

Youth culture was forever transformed when The Beatles stormed onto *The Ed Sullivan Show* in 1964.

When the World Wide Web enabled the first free transfer of digital information in the early 1990s, it was a Kansas Moment.

And when people first lay eyes on their newborn child, they realize that everything in their life has changed.

We cannot control when these Kansas Moments happen to us, but we can select the kind of glasses we use to look at them as they unfold. The choice is between a pair of glasses with a competitive lens or a pair with a creative lens.

"

The beginning of knowledge is the discovery of something we do not understand.

"

Frank Herbert

Competition is embedded into the very fabric of modern life. We strive for good grades in school to get into a good university, so as to get a good job in a company that functions like a hierarchy, promising promotions to new levels if we do well. Add in everything from loyalty programmes to Olympic medal denominations (bronze, silver and gold) to social media brands that reward views, likes and retweets and you end up with a life that often looks and feels like one long competition. In a competitive world, you can either win or lose. A Kansas Moment is either a huge opportunity or a threat if you wear competitive glasses.

Creation is something completely different. It is about bringing something into this world – an idea, a work of art, an invention – that we have not seen before. It does not function along a win-lose spectrum because it is so different from what we are used to. This causes bewilderment, ignorance and anger. Think about the number of artists who have had their creations belittled by the establishment because what they made – abstract cubes or an unmade bed – was so different from what came before. A competitive person will ignore everything that does not fit their imagined path they will take to reach more extraordinary highs. A person wearing creative glasses will be neutral – or, to use a more philosophical word, 'stoic,' which means enduring hardship without succumbing to it.

In the famous parable, a Chinese farmer loses a horse but only says "maybe" when his neighbours complain about the misfortune. When the lost horse returns the next day, bringing a flock of wild horses with it, the neighbours congratulate the farmer and say, "That's great, isn't it?" The farmer again says, "maybe."

When the farmer's son tries to tame one of the wild horses, he breaks his leg, and again the neighbours are regretful and say, "That's too bad."

The farmer says, "maybe."

When conscription officers come to the village looking for soldiers to enrol, they reject the farmer's son because of his broken leg. The neighbours rejoice and tell the farmer that this is very good.

The farmer, again, says only the word, "maybe."

Like the Chinese farmer, we rarely know what it is we are looking at and what its long-term consequences will be. Happiness research has shown that people can suffer all kinds of adversity – losing limbs or loved ones – and return to the same state of happiness, even a higher state, over time. Likewise, we can believe that if a certain event were to happen – winning the lottery or an Academy Award – we would be forever grateful and enjoy an elevated state of well-being for the rest of our lives, only to be back to our boring old selves after a few months.

Using a creative lens is about accepting this sense of not knowing, and suspending judgement.

A Kansas Moment – of which you will have many in life – is neither good nor bad; it just is.

CHAPTER 5
THE GROUCHO
MARX PRINCIPLE

A strange and unexpected thought took shape in Stig's head when he saw his family washed away by a tsunami wave in Thailand. Holding on to a palm tree for dear life, he saw his wife and two infant sons disappear in the deadly waters yet thought to himself: "I will create a new family."

They were three of over 200,000 victims of the horrific 2004 disaster that affected more than a dozen countries around the Indian Ocean.

Stig buried his family back in Sweden and made time to grieve, but he also had a clear goal: "Within three years, I will have created a new family," he repeated to himself and others.

This was a provocative statement to many. Stig, somehow, did not correspond to preconceived notions of sorrow and grief. Losing our spouse and all of our children is a nightmare too bleak to fathom and, were it to happen, we imagine that we would be lost and broken forever.

Stig broke the rules of grief.

"

We cannot change anything unless we accept it. Condemnation does not liberate, it oppresses.

"

Carl Jung

The comedian Groucho Marx famously said: "Those are my principles, and if you don't like them... well, I have others." The crux of the joke is that personal principles are considered rigid and holy – why else would we call them principles? – but Marx treats them as something flexible that can be quickly abandoned to fit a specific purpose. The reason we laugh, however, is not because Marx is breaking a taboo but because his words illustrate something deeply human. We hold on tightly – to principles, rules of grief, ideals and dogma – but let go lightly if the circumstances change. Marx is showing us a life skill masquerading as a joke.

Infidelity is an awful thing to imagine in a marriage, which is why we swear variations of the oath that we will love the other person, and only them, for as long as we live. However, modern marriages are characterized by an unrealistic paradox. As Belgian psychotherapist Esther Perel points out, we simultaneously seek novelty and relationship stability. This, Perel explains, is one of the reasons that marriages increasingly end in divorce either because one party has broken the once sacred wedding vows or because they want to break them.

In her book about infidelity, *The State of Affairs*, Perel offers couples in a crisis a solution similar to Marx's life skill and Stig's broken rule: "Your first marriage is over; do you want to create a second one together?" Instead of trying to patch up and mend what was broken or suffer in purgatory, she urges her clients to build new relationships from scratch – but with each other.

Perel's advice, Marx's principle and Stig's response to grief can be seen as a kind of cheating in the game of life. Shouldn't the breaking of expectations, vows and principles be met by guilt, pain and suffering? Instead, this breaking is better thought of as a kind of freedom to be explored – the third way, or a compromise between binary extremes. Not 'either/or' but 'what if?'

It is a new model in which to live and love in our complex world.

When we spend our lives floating on a self-delusional cloud, we simplify things into binary options. They are either good or bad, stupid or clever, black or white.

The cartoon series *South Park* invented the ManBearPig – a fearsome blend of three creatures – to illustrate how society debates climate change: Does it exist? Is it real? Should we worry? This ingenious narrative trick captures the essence of one of society's most significant debates in the 21st century: How worried should we be about rising carbon dioxide levels in the atmosphere?

On one side, we have people who see the end of the world as we know it, and no sacrifice is too great to avoid it. Conversely, we have people who shrug and argue that what we see is naturally occurring and that any significant intervention would cause more harm than good.

Polarized debates get their lifeblood from our unwillingness to move away from our position. To change your mind is akin to conceding defeat – unworthy and shameful. Yet societal progress is characterized by long, fierce debates resolved by practical solutions. As *Chapter 11, The Alien Way*, will explore further, in the short run, energy debates are focusing on present solutions – nuclear or renewables – but new technologies will create unexpected ways to generate electricity in the long run.

We hold on tightly but let go lightly when new inventions help us to resolve the deadlock.

CHAPTER 6
BREAKING THE
LOOP OF DENIAL

In the movies, characters get one moment of insight and, with a musical crescendo in the background, we see how they change their minds in a few seconds. In reality, denial is not an informational problem but a motivational one. It relies on three internal forces: self-rationalization, false prophecy and convenience – or laziness, to use a more accurate word. Self-rationalization is where we tell ourselves that our bad marriage or poor physical shape is not that bad; just look at what others are going through. False prophecy happens when we make up stories about the future to feel good about the present without realizing it. Finally, laziness is putting off things and procrastinating because we do not have the urge to get them done today. We need more than one moment of insight to break these three forces.

Knowledge is just dead information. It is based on data gathered in the past – in a course you took last year or on scientific measurements made decades ago. Pluto was once a planet, and diseases were caused by the level of black bile or phlegm being out of balance in the body. New information kills old knowledge. Our values and prejudices will similarly atrophy. Some make us feel good; others give us a sense of meaning or belonging. When they are challenged, we tend to fight back and hold on, preferring the convenience of convictions to the wasteland of bewilderment. This is why the definition of a crisis is not just a moment of change or a turning point but a time of intense difficulty. New, unexpected, shocking information challenges our old selves and beliefs. Our very core is attacked. Can this blow be softened? Can we learn to deal with crises in a better way?

The next section of this book – Part II: Battling New Realities – will deal with the outpouring of emotion we feel when the veil of denial is lifted and we are forced to face a new reality. Before that, this chapter will introduce the concept of 'unlearning', which is a valuable tool in our journey from denial to acceptance. Learning was once a one-way street – you went to school for a few years, acquired a few skills, and had a lifelong profession on a farm or factory. Today, human longevity and ingenuity have thrown a spanner in the works and knowledge's half-life has decreased significantly. Learning has become a two-way street that involves putting new things in and taking old items out. Or, to quote a medieval Catholic cardinal, Thomas Wolsey: "Be careful what you put inside your head because you might never get it out of there."

Unlearning sounds easy in theory, but it is challenging because knowledge is heavily intertwined with our identity – unless we are asked to point out the cognitive shortcomings of others. We are quick to see and suggest what opinions and ideas others should change – whether during dinner-table discussions or in commentary threads on social media. This is hypocritical, of course, but also helpful. It shows us that unlearning is not difficult because we lack data or contradictory ideas but because we are unused to the idea of changing our minds. Therefore, step one on the road to unlearning is to practise it in small doses.

"

To see what is in front of one's nose needs a constant struggle.

"

George Orwell

An ancient myth of uncertain origin tells of a king who vows to kill his son by crushing him with a large rock in a fit of rage. When the anger subsides, the king panics because he does not want to kill his son, but he cannot be seen as weak by breaking his promise. An adviser resolves the dilemma by suggesting that the giant rock is split into a thousand pebbles. The king can keep his contract and the son survives. What can kill you in a large dose is harmless in micro-doses. The same goes for poison, drugs and ideas that contradict your personal beliefs.

If you are going to break, or at least weaken, the three internal forces that keep you in a loop of denial (self-rationalization, false prophecy and convenience), you should expose them to a steady stream of small, preferably non-threatening questions. What activity can I dedicate ten minutes to today? What is the very opposite of what I feel and think right now? What if I'm wrong and reality is even better than I thought? We can call them micro-doses of enlightenment. They will make for poor cinema since there is not one moment of clarity with John Williams-style string music playing in the background. Instead, they will make your mind a bit more agile and stretchy – the first line of defense against the surprises in store for all of us.

"

Just because you're strong enough to handle the pain, doesn't mean you deserve it "

Trent Shelton

PART TWO

BATTLING
NEW REALITIES

CHAPTER 7
WHY DOES IT
ALWAYS RAIN
CHEESE ON ME?

"It's so unfair!"

These words are an immediate instinctive response to any big or small disaster that befalls us. We were living life blissfully unaware of hidden potholes, stock market weaknesses or tumour growths and then – often in an instant – they intruded. Why did it have to happen to us?

There are two problems with this line of reasoning: the "why" and the "to us." This chapter will deal with the human inclination to live our lives in the passive voice and the so-called just-world fallacy.

The idea that supernatural forces beyond our control govern human lives was wholly uncontroversial for thousands of years of human civilization. Gods and other spiritual deities kept us in check with esoteric rules that were designed to keep us on the straight and narrow. When we fell ill or suffered an accident, or the summer harvest was wrecked by drought or flood, it was seen as a sign that the gods were angry with us and that we had broken one or more of said esoteric rules. There are many things to laugh at or criticize in a world guided by superstition, but at least it gives humans some sense of individual agency about controlling their fate. This cannot be said for the prevalent modern belief that stuff happens to us, not because of us.

Why was I left by my wife? Why has mainstream media been transformed into a mouthpiece for extremists? Why were mortgage rates increased just as I bought a new apartment? And why am I always funnelled into the slowest queue? These are just a few common complaints, some more serious than others, that use the passive voice. Things are happening to us, not because of us. We are hapless victims of some loosely connected conspiracy. When our denial slowly dissipates, victimhood sets in, and if this were a spiritual self-help book with a title like *You Are Not a Victim*, it would have urged you to do breathing exercises and tell yourself over and over that you own your life and your narrative. This book, however, will tell you that you are mostly correct in seeing yourself at the helpless end of life's forces. But you are 5% wrong.

Freud – not the bearded Austrian whose self-invented theories of the mind laid the foundation for psychotherapy but his grand-daughter Sophie, a professor and psychiatric social worker based in the United States – used to say that we have only 5% liberty in how we control our lives. This does not belittle individual agency – 5% is quite a lot. Re-examine the rhetorical question of despair – "why me?" – and consider how the answer changes if you have 5% of the responsibility for your spouse leaving you.

It can also be helpful to look at how the airline industry explains disasters using Swiss cheese as a metaphor. In the tragic and thankfully rare instances that a plane crashes, it is through a confluence of factors, not one single cause. The captain was a little sloppy, some debris was on the runway, a software patch was missing on the plane's inflight computer, and, finally, a gust of wind blew at precisely the wrong time. Each factor can be viewed as a slice of cheese with holes in it. If you dropped each piece on the ground at random on top of each other, there would be a slight chance of all the holes lining up all the way through the pile. In most cases, the runway debris or gust of wind go by without anyone noticing, but in rare, unfortunate instances, they conspire to cause an accident.

Every day contains more possibilities than we can fathom, let alone take advantage of. It is, so to speak, raining Swiss cheese slices around us all the time, but most of them miss those already on the ground or land atop each other without the holes lining up. And when they *do* line up, we should blame ourselves for approximately 5% of the consequences – no more, no less.

The symbol of justice is a blindfolded woman holding a sword in one hand and a pair of scales in the other. The blindfold conveys the idea that everyone should be equal before the law, the sword symbolizes punishment for the guilty, and the scales illustrate the notion that justice is about symmetry between crime and consequences. People tend to have the same concept of symmetry in their lives – we should get back what we put in. This is why our reaction is so visceral when something terrible and unexpected happens. In this sense, we suffer from the just-world fallacy.

"
We're living a fairy tale someone else wrote.
"

Melissa de la Cruz

The human fascination with competitive sports is believed to derive from the sense of closure that we get from a match between two participants. Competitive sports allow us to witness a real battle with a resolution in real time, and in an environment where the participants strive towards fairness and where cheating, anabolic steroids and corrupt referees are frowned upon. This is attractive because a level playing field of this kind is so rare in life and society. Wars end with two losers or long-term simmering conflict after the shooting ends. Families have long-held grudges against each other or some other entity they believe has wronged them. Crimes remain unsolved and societies are mired in inequality, absolute and relative. In short, we live in a deeply unfair world. This fact proves notoriously tricky for human beings to rise above. We prefer to watch sports and tell stories where there is a clear and symmetrical link between input and output. The better team won, and the character with more noble intentions – Robin Hood, not Prince John – reached their goals. If only life were as simple.

We live our lives and craft our beliefs with the goal that what we put in should pay good dividends. What we eat and drink, how hard we work or exercise, and the general goodness we spread around us should somehow all add up to a kind of VIP treatment from life itself. However, this commonly held notion is, unfortunately, a recipe for disappointment. The belief that the world is just is a romantic notion and a motivator to do good, but it is not a description of how the world works. Bad things happen to good people, and evil people can enjoy earthly rewards. Some high achievers live lives riddled with anxiety and a lack of self-worth, whereas some downright lazy people live blissfully. There is no justice. It is tempting to add a 'but' or 'however' here, but we will all just have to live with the fact that the world at large and life itself are not crafted narratives but random patterns of cheese slices.

CHAPTER 8
A SIMPLE RECIPE
FOR DEFUSING
EMOTIONS AND
HARVESTING LUCK

Revenge is a poison you take, hoping someone else dies from it.

When Olle's wife cheated on him with another man, he did what any self-respecting human burning with rage and jealousy would: he went to see the other man armed with a hammer.

But things did not turn out as Olle had expected. His rival opened the door dressed in a silk scarf and invited Olle in for cognac and cigars. It was the beginning of a beautiful friendship.

That is, if the song "Trubbel" (Swedish for 'trouble') is to be believed.

Written by Swedish folk singer Olle Adolphson in the early 1960s, this song's lyrics have a particularly Nordic quality. Instead of hot-blooded revenge and punishment, adultery leads to friendship. More specifically, what the song illustrates is the inverse relationship between time and emotion. This chapter will explore how feelings can be considered physical forces and dealt with accordingly. We will also get unexpected advice from a whisky advertisement.

When something terrible and unexpected happens in our lives, we risk falling into a downward spiral of negativity. The depth and speed depend on the event's gravity and how much of our narrative has been derailed. A crisis is not a precise description of reality but a subjective experience. Shame, resentment, anger and depression are considered normal reactions to a terminal disease but overreactions if someone steals your parking spot right before your eyes. Time, however, is an equally effective tool in both cases.

Feelings are created by chemicals – what we call anger is the result of chemical compounds rushing around in our blood – but they behave like physical forces. When an object is set in motion, some kind of counterforce is needed to stop it. When it comes to human emotions, this counterforce is time. Taking a deep breath and counting to ten is usually enough when someone steals your parking lot. But what if your whole life has fallen apart?

When John Walker's father died in the early 1800s, his family sold their farm and invested the small proceeds in a wine shop in western Scotland. Walker himself did not drink alcohol but started dealing in hard spirits, such as gin and rum. His homemade whisky was particularly popular and his son, Alexander, began marketing it after his father passed away, naming it after his father's nickname, Johnnie Walker. Soon after, the company began to use a mascot, the Striding Man, as its symbol. The slogan became "Keep Walking." This is not only a famous saying but also excellent advice for disarming emotional intensity. Our emotional system is armed for real-time situations due to what is most likely evolutionary residue from when we were threatened by lions on a savannah long ago. However, even though your whole system is boiling, somebody stealing your parking spot is not a life-or-death situation. Keep walking.

The same advice works for much graver situations. A timeless example tells of a man who suffered tremendously and when asked how he was, he replied: "I'm going through hell!" His friend simply replied, "Well, keep on going. That is no place to stop!"

This is contrarian advice. People have a propensity to act, and we live in a culture that celebrates doing things. There is a reason that Nike's iconic slogan is "Just Do It!" not "Just Think About It!"

But doing without thinking is a recipe for disaster. Stories about adultery often begin with the words "we were both drunk." Any police officer can also attest that a disproportionate number of crimes happen because the criminal has been drinking. It was long ago popular to view alcohol as an inhibitor that slowed down your ability to react. This view has changed, and it is now believed that the reason alcohol causes accidents is that it impairs our ability to anticipate what will happen next. It forces the drinker to live too much in the present, which is why drivers overreact to immediate stimuli – such as somebody crossing the road or headlights appearing in the opposite lane – when they have been drinking.

Furthermore, alcohol is like a teleportation device that transports energy from tomorrow morning so that you can dance better in the bar tonight – or gain physical strength when someone has been hitting on your girlfriend and revenge is called for.

Keep walking. Drink less.

If you want to annoy a wealthy person – why not? – tell them they just had luck on their side. The more successful people get, the more they ascribe their success to inner strength and their own skill set. We call the ancient ruler Alexander the Great, not Alexander the Lucky.

In reality, turning points in our lives tend to be governed by luck – of the good or bad kind.

Sticking with kings, consider the assassination attempt on Mohammed Zahir Shah, king of Afghanistan, in Italy in 1991. An Al-Qaeda terrorist posing as a journalist was invited to interview the king and stabbed him several times. The king had recently stopped smoking cigars on his doctor's orders, but had switched to cigarillos because he could not kick the habit altogether. A metal tin containing these slim, brown sticks of tobacco was in his breast pocket, and this stopped the knife from reaching his vital organs. He survived and the terrorist was arrested.

This kind of thing happens to us daily – usually not in the shape of botched assassination attempts but as serendipitous situations where unexpected things collide.

When the pop group Dire Straits recorded a new album on the Caribbean island of Montserrat in the early 1980s, a microphone placed in front of a speaker slipped out of the bearings on the stand and came to rest pointing towards the floor instead. When lead singer Mark Knopfler played his guitar through the amplifier, it created a new and unique noise that became the signature sound on the number-one hit "Money for Nothing."

When biochemist Jennifer Doudna accidentally met microbiologist Emmanuelle Charpentier at a conference in Puerto Rico, they had no idea they would jointly win the Nobel Prize in chemistry less than a decade later.

"

Life doesn't happen to you; it happens for you.

"

Jim Carrey

A life governed by luck is not a call to resignation. You cannot control everything that will happen to you, but you can control how you view and use what happens. And what you put in. This is known as the input–output effect. Modern hustle culture places far too much emphasis on the inputs. We are told – by numerous social media personalities and self-help gurus – that we should rise early, exercise daily, work hard and live healthily. Excessive focus on this side tends to be followed by disillusionment when luck – of the wrong kind – has its way with you.

The output and result should govern what you do and how you think.

Let us take the composer Andrew Lloyd Webber as an example.

In the 1970s, just after he had reached mainstream success with the musical *Jesus Christ Superstar*, Lloyd Webber was approached to adapt the Thomas the Tank Engine stories into a TV series. After two years of creating a pilot, the project was abandoned because the financiers doubted its potential.

Let us assume Lloyd Webber put effort into this and that the pilot episode was good. Yet the output was a failure. What do you do if you have a good input but a lousy output? You keep walking.

In a luck-driven world, frequency yields rewards – a statement that is valid for both lottery tickets and creative work.

Around the same time, Lloyd Webber heard Earl Jordan, an American soul singer, who could sing three notes at once. The unique sound inspired him to write and record "Engine of Love" with Jordan. It was a complete flop.

Keep walking.

Finally, Lloyd Webber had written some musical pieces for an American TV show that would put a spin on the tale of Cinderella. But, instead of humans, Cinderella, her sisters and Prince Charming would all be portrayed as trains.

The project sank without a trace.

With three failures in three attempts, Lloyd Webber might easily have given up. But instead, he combined the three failures into a new musical called *Starlight Express*. It became one of the longest-running musicals in London and Broadway ever and bought joy to millions around the world.

If your input is terrible, nothing helps.

If you put the hours in and apply your creative thought, luck will find you sooner or later.

Keep walking.

CHAPTER 9
LONG LIVE
SUFFERING

Imagine that you have been tasked by some supreme being with writing a recipe for a good life, with 'good' meaning 'enjoyable.'

You would most likely include sunny days by the seaside, some favourite meals, songs and wine (but not too much), and lovemaking, possibly by the beach. Et voilà – an enjoyable life!

Imagine then that this supreme being scans your answers and asks you how much suffering you want to add into the mix.

Surely you must have misheard the supreme being, you think.

It assures you that you have not.

There are many examples of wilful suffering – from enduring steaming hot saunas and soaking in ice baths to eating chicken vindaloo or rotten herring (a Swedish delicacy). But there is something meaningful in the kind of suffering that we do not seek out but that rather seeks us out.

A famous study conducted by researchers at Stanford University found significant differences in how people perceive 'a happy life' and 'a meaningful life.' Suffering and the worry, stress and anxiety that go along with it made the study participants less happy but contributed to a higher sense of meaningfulness.

To put this in the words of Seneca, a philosopher: "things that were hard to bear are sweet to remember."

Any attic or self-storage facility is a testament to the human inability to make accurate predictions. The expensive Peloton exercise bike was a great idea when your New Year's resolutions were still intact, but it is now gathering dust. This optimism bias makes us overestimate our abilities and underestimate negative consequences. In her book *Aftermath*, Canadian author Rachel Cusk describes how divorce is caused by this inability to predict the future accurately: "Modern family life, with its relentless jollity, its entirely unfounded optimism, its reliance not on God or economics but the principles of love, fails to recognize – and to take precaution against – the human need for war."

It is fashionable for political leaders to say that things – pandemics, inflation, war – were utterly unexpected. In reality, optimism bias makes them challenging to predict, but not impossible. Optimism bias makes us one-eyed as future thinkers.

Seeking out suffering means opening both eyes to the possibilities – good and bad – in our lives and societies.

And especially in our organizations.

**Nature is so exact,
it hurts exactly as
much as it is worth,
so in a way one relishes
the pain, I think.
If it didn't matter,
it wouldn't matter.**

Julian Barnes

When groups are formed – from the Spice Girls to the technology company Apple – they tend to go through certain stages. They tend to be happy, curious and clueless when they begin. Then, as roles are designated and goals are set, they go through a period of 'storming,' as the psychologist Bruce Tuckman named it. Conflict, arguments and fighting characterize this stage. Many groups, like the Spice Girls, do not make it past this stage, but the ones that do find that their level of trust and loyalty is higher and they are better equipped to reach their goals. Fighting, in other words, fills a valuable purpose in forming solid teams. Chris Martin, frontman of the successful rock band Coldplay, explains tension's value in the group: "if there were no tension in the violin's strings, it wouldn't play."

Suffering was for a long time positioned as masculine and paired with macho quotes along the lines that "whatever doesn't kill you only makes you stronger." However, this view has changed over the past decades. Suffering does not make you stronger because you become bulletproof and more robust; quite the opposite. It can make you more open and empathetic. The late bestselling author and award-winner Hilary Mantel is a good example. She suffered from debilitating pain in her twenties and the doctors could not help her. She finally conducted her own research and found that she had severe endometriosis. The surgery needed to alleviate her pain left her unable to have children by the age of 27. Whilst the illness made her suffer, it also made her a better author, as one of her many obituary's pointed out: " Hilary Mantel's art was infused with her pain. She worked her experience until it became the corporeal substrate of her fiction."

There is a way to invite suffering into your life: making 'uphill decisions.' When you face a dilemma, always choose the path that seems more difficult, even painful. Just like when you play a computer game, obstacles and enemies are signs that you are going in the right direction. This is the literal meaning of the word 'passion.' Contrary to the cliche that 'passionate' has become (applied to anything from foods we love to tasks we are good at), passion means suffering, burning and sacrificing. In a world of abundance, when you avoid suffering, you are wilfully abstaining from things that have greater value. In a world where people prefer to avoid pain, withstanding it brings rewards.

Don't waste suffering.

CHAPTER 10
THE SECOND
MOUNTAIN

Life is a journey to the tops of two very different mountains. The first mountain constitutes our first venture, where we go to school, find something we would like to do in life, get a job, fall in love, and go on to have a career, a family or both. The first mountain is all about self-realization.

But then something happens. We fall or are kicked off the first mountain. We become ill or are fired. We get a divorce or suffer an accident. That is when we discover the second mountain.

As the creator of the metaphor, columnist David Brooks, points out: "people on the second mountain have made firm commitments to one or all of these things: a vocation, a spouse and family, a philosophy or faith, a community, a duty, making a promise to something without expecting a reward." If the first mountain was all 'me,' the second is all 'we.'"

This chapter focuses on the secret places that lie ahead of us in the fog of the future and that we can start exploring once our emotional turmoil subsides.

> **Midway along the journey of our life. I came around and found myself now searching. Through a dark wood, the right way blurred and lost.**

Dante's *Inferno*

"The thought of those officers and men as well as others who have fallen in the fields of battle, those who died at their posts of duty, or those who met with untimely death and all their bereaved families, pains our heart night and day." These words are taken from Japanese Emperor Hirohito's surrender broadcast at the end of the Second World War. The speech, broadcast on public radio on 15 August 1945, was less than five minutes long and declared Japan's unconditional surrender. Emperor Hirohito spoke of suffering ahead but of staying strong in the face of adversity. Above all, he wanted to end the hell of war, especially since the United States had "begun to employ a new and most cruel bomb, the power of which to do damage is, indeed, incalculable, taking the toll of many innocent lives." He ended by asking Japan's citizens to devote themselves "to construction for the future" and "keep pace with the progress of the world."

The transformation that lay ahead was remarkable. Japan could refocus its engineers, who had previously built warplanes and battleships, into designing and constructing the first and, to this day, most admired high-speed rail system in the world: the Shinkansen bullet train. An entire society had been able to find a second mountain.

Detroit-born musician Mike Posner was standing alone at a show by the DJ Avicii in Ibiza. He was miserable. His music career had stalled, leaving him feeling sad, lost and utterly alone among hundreds of screaming fans. He hoped he would feel some belonging, but it was not happening. Someone in the crowd offered Posner a pill, which he unwisely swallowed. He "felt like hell" the following day but chronicled this time of sadness in a ballad called "I Took a Pill in Ibiza." A remixed, upbeat version of the song became a top-ten hit in nearly 30 countries worldwide. "People are having happy times out of my sadness," Posner later reflected.

Posner's words show why art is the most valuable human activity. When Eric Clapton's young son died in a tragic accident in the early 1990s, he used the sorrow to write "Tears in Heaven," one of his most played and beloved songs. Art, and human creativity at large, is a machine that transforms negative emotions – grief, anger, loneliness, heartbreak – into something beautiful. It is the second mountain embodied.

The word 'crisis' comes from *krisis* in ancient Greek. It is now commonly used to refer to something terrible and unexpected that happens to us, but the word originally meant a decision – a point of separation that created a new direction. As *Chapter 8, A Simple Recipe for Defusing Emotions and Harvesting Luck,* began to explore, a crisis is not something that happens to you; it is a situation where you can make a choice.

When Ole Kirk Christiansen's carpentry business burned to the ground in 1924, he decided to expand instead of calling it quits. Born as one of ten children in a low-income family in Jutland, rural Denmark, he had worked as a carpenter since age 14 and on the family farm since age six. His decision to expand paid dividends, and in the early 1930s he had a company of two dozen employees. His wife passed away, leaving him a widower with four children to care for. Then came the Great Depression, and nobody could afford to buy Christiansen's carpentry, so he had to fire all his employees.

He decided to use his skills to build toys, believing them to be recession-proof. He called his new endeavour Lego, after the Danish words for 'play well' (*leg godt*).

The toys enabled the company to survive and grow during the depression and Second World War, during which the Nazis occupied Denmark. But then there was a second fire – the new factory Christiansen had built to produce his wooden toys burned to the ground along with all the drawings and designs he had made for his products. For the first time, Christiansen felt like giving up, but he also thought he owed it to his employees to keep going.

A shortage of wood in the wake of the war meant that Lego had to start making things with plastic instead. When a new kind of plastic – ABS – was launched in the early 1950s, Lego realized that they could make toys that were both hard and soft at the same time – hard enough to build things but soft enough to easily connect plastic pieces together.

The Lego brick was patented in January 1958.

Find your second mountain.

"

What a time
to be alive!

"

British coping mechanism,
circa 2020s

PART THREE

THE LAND OF
THE NEW

CHAPTER 11
THE ALIEN WAY

No records reveal what the Italian poet Petrarch felt when he discovered Cicero's ancient letters in Verona Cathedral in 1345. The crumbling parchments were over a thousand years old and written in Ancient Latin. When Petrarch started deciphering them, he realized how much more sophisticated the world of ancient Rome had been compared with 14th century Europe and how far society had crumbled in the dark ages since. Using this ancient wisdom, Petrarch became one of the originators of the Renaissance, a period that would change the world forever. It laid the foundation for modernity, rational thought, art, discovery and science. It would not have happened had the world not gone through a deadly pandemic.

The prevailing theory when the Black Death struck Europe in the mid-1300s was that three planets had aligned and caused pestilence in the air. The modern scientific theory is that rats from Asia carried the bacteria with them on trading ships, which is why the plague struck Mediterranean seaports first. It went on to wreak havoc across the continent over the coming decades, killing millions and destroying villages, households and economies.

It also changed how we view the world. Religion lost part of its grip and command over the masses. The widespread death made people think more about their present life and what to do with it rather than abstractions of an afterlife. Most importantly, it opened the door to new ways of thinking and viewing the world. This is why the Renaissance is named after the idea of rebirth. The world was reborn and adopted a new direction after decades, even centuries, of suffering.

Politics is many things, but the Iron Chancellor of Germany, Otto von Bismarck, summarized it best: "Politics is the art of the possible, the attainable – the art of the next best." As voters, we wait in vain for inspiring visions of the future and fail to grasp that politicians dabble in the present. Should we invest in renewables as a power source or fossil fuels? Should we tax the rich or force people to work longer hours? Democracies are deadlocked in a polarized either/or trap.

Might aliens offer us a solution? A strange question indeed that takes some explanation. In May 2017, a computer program defeated the reigning champion Ke Jie in the ancient board game *Go*. This is one of many examples where machines have excelled at and surpassed human gaming skills – from chess to *Space Invaders*. What sets this example apart is a comment made about the computer program itself: "It doesn't play like a human, and it doesn't play like a program. It plays in a third, almost alien, way." The computer showed us entirely new, strange ways of mastering a game that is over 2,000 years old.

The Alien Way entails being open to new, previously unthinkable solutions. It is the antidote to entrenched polarization. Take political debates about electricity as an example. People favouring decarbonized alternatives such as solar or wind power hate the proponents of nuclear power or carbon capture technology because, they say, we simply cannot waste any time saving our dying planet. On the other hand, the nuclear and coal advocates argue that the proponents of renewables are naive about the effect of these power sources and say that we will wreck the economy without saving the planet.

The Alien Way can break the deadlock by revealing future electricity sources. One example is piezo power, which involves harvesting human movement, such as people walking on a sidewalk. Another is genetic manipulation, which involves copying the hereditary qualities of other species, such as the bioluminescent DNA of the kitefin shark. This sea creature can glow in the dark and if we could paste its DNA into building materials, we could create electricity-free light. The Alien Way is not an answer in and of itself but a method that may be used to open up horizons for the future – a kind of instant renaissance.

Do not waste a crisis. Although crises are distressing to go through, they can sharpen your senses and open your eyes to the previously unseen.

In the mid-1950s, just when he was about to become a father for the first time, John Naisbitt ran out of money and could not pay for his college tuition. Wanting to provide for his new family, he dropped out and started work as a PR consultant and speech writer. A decade later, he was tasked with measuring how successful President Lyndon B. Johnson had been in his policies and assessing the national mood in the United States. This was long before polls were conducted in real time, so Naisbitt had to invent a new method. He simply went to the nearest newsstand and bought as many newspapers from as many different places as he could find. This opened his eyes to what was going on in and around America. He crafted a methodology based on accurate newspaper reading and hired a group of assistants to help him go through the content. It did not go well. His marriage ended and the company went bust in the late 1970s. Naisbitt himself filed for personal bankruptcy. When he tried to withhold some small artworks from the authorities, he was convicted of bankruptcy fraud and sentenced to community service and probation.

> **What happens after the Black Death? It's like a wind – fresh air coming in, the fresh air of common sense.**
>
> Gianna Pomata

He was broke, divorced and living in a basement. 'Rock bottom' would describe the situation well.

He started over, this time focusing mainly on giving talks about what he had learned from scouring newspapers for over 20 years. He met and married Patricia Aburdene, a journalist, who suggested he put all of his thoughts into a book. He had called his method 'content analysis', which would have been quite a boring book title. He settled on the punchier *Megatrends* instead and the book was published in 1982.

It became a global phenomenon and made Naisbitt a rich man. He was able to travel the world and advise political leaders and business executives. His renaissance had begun in that basement apartment when he had nothing left to lose.

Find the alien way.

CHAPTER 12
FEED THE WELL

If you had been a fly on the wall in the late American musician Tom Petty's household, you would very likely have concluded that he was lazy. He would spend his days watching Turner Classic Movies on the TV and listening to new music on the radio. Not how you might imagine productivity for a world-class songwriter, but you would be wrong to assume Petty was being idle. His daughter Adria would later call this activity "feeding the well": "He would feed the well with only this good information and take all the rest away. He didn't take a lot of noise and negativity into his diet." Inside all of us is a well of thoughts, knowledge and inspiration. It will run dry if we don't feed it. And if we feed it with bad information, it will poison our minds.

One of the first maps of the internet was created in May 1973. The ARPA Network Logical Map featured just over 40 interconnected computers. Those few dozen computers were the entire World Wide Web, although that name would take another 20 years to appear.

In contrast, if you search for the words 'ARPA Network Logical Map, 1973' through any search engine today, you will get tens of thousands of results. The world's access to information has exploded in around half a century.

Imagination and fiction make up more than three quarters of our real life.

Simone Weil

There have been numerous positive effects of this abundant, free information, but what about the harmful effects?

First of all, it has made us less informed, not more. How so?

With the rise of abundant, easily accessible information, solitary thinking became less attractive, as did walking to and physically searching for texts in archives and libraries. Our opinions – about ourselves and others – were able to roam free.

Imagine for a moment that you have a fixation that people of a particular political spectrum – take liberals as an example – are all idiots. The phrase 'liberals are idiots' will generate a myriad of results, many supporting your belief. If you believe all Swedish people are idiots, you are bound to find thousands of articles supporting your claim.

And so on.

Beliefs - especially the outrageous kind - were strengthened in this digital echo chamber.

Secondly, the level of connectivity and the speed with which information can spread means that we overreact to stimuli. Even the smallest rumours can trigger panic, wild speculation and stock market crashes. Martijn Verbove, a digital specialist, likens this to an "over-reactive immune system." This makes it hard to accurately gauge truth and importance. In other words, it has become more challenging to discern what's important in the steady stream of noise.

This is why Tom Petty's ritual of feeding the well matters more than ever.

When calories became abundant in the late 1900s, we realized that eating whatever we wanted all of the time was a bad idea. The same is true for information.

But what does all of this have to do with coming out of the other side of a crisis?

When we are under pressure in the midst of a crisis, we retreat to the familiar. We stop exploring new things. We eat comfort foods instead of sous-vide gourmet cuisine. When the Covid-19 pandemic hit the world like a sledgehammer in the spring of 2020, we started hoarding toilet paper, retreating to our primal instincts. In this way, a crisis can act as a gravitational force that shuts off our curiosity and switches on our need for convenience. In the aftermath of a crisis, we need to reboot our information intake.

We need to feed the well.

CHAPTER 13
LOOK
ELSEWHERE

One of the most effective ways of seeing things and spotting opportunities is to use a method called 'Page 2 learning.' In the words of Sahil Bloom, the investor who coined the expression, "Page 1 is the first page on Google or the front page of the newspaper. Page 1 is what's readily available to the masses. But everyone reads Page 1." There are no unique opportunities if you read what everybody else is reading. To find them, you have to go to page 2. You have to look where nobody else is looking. Exciting things are hidden in the folds of reality.

The Bee Gees had a first career as a folksy boy band in the UK in the 1960s. With albums such as *Spicks and Specks* and *Horizontal*, they toured the world and scored hit singles. However, they decided to break up when their fortunes started to point downward in the early 1970s. They therefore went their separate ways. However, their strong bond as brothers led them to reform after a few years, and they relocated to Miami to find new inspiration.

Southern Florida is a mix of beaches, marshland and archipelagos reached only by bridges that can be raised and lowered to accommodate big ships and yachts. When the brothers were not trying to record new music in the studio, they would drive around on the bridges of Miami. That was when they noticed something interesting. As the car travelled over the joints in the bridges, the tyres would make a rhythmic chunka-chunka sound. It sounded unique and upbeat. Since they had dabbled mainly in ballads and were tired of the format, they decided to use the sound as a drum beat. It laid the foundation for a new sound and the unique disco rhythm that would conquer the world over the coming decade. You can hear the chunka-chunka sound if you play the opening to "Jive Talking'," the first hit single of their second career.

In evolutionary biology, there is a concept called 'exaptation'. Elisabeth Vrba, a German palaeontologist, has researched how certain traits and features of species that evolve for a particular purpose can be used for something completely different. An example would be feathers on birds that evolved for thermal regulation but later enabled birds to fly. When the Bee Gees used car tyres travelling over Miami bridges to create a new drum rhythm, it was an example of creative exaptation.

This is why inventors often look to adjacent areas and industries to find solutions to their problems.

Compeed, the blister plaster, was invented when somebody tried putting a piece of colostomy bag adhesive on their feet and found it worked marvellously.

The Nintendo Wii was invented because engineers used motion-sensitive airbag computer chips instead of regular gaming computer chips.

" Innovation happens when ideas have sex. "

Matt Ridley

When Steven Spielberg was preparing to make *Jurassic Park*, he struggled with how to convey the sheer scale of the prehistoric creatures in a cinematic and captivating manner. Simply shooting a giant T-Rex next to a tiny human risked undermining the sense of awe, wonder and terror that a genetically resurrected prehistoric monster might inspire. Spielberg had learned this almost two decades earlier while working on *Jaws*, where the threat of an unseen shark is far scarier than the shark itself.

The answer came to him from the 1970s funk band Earth, Wind & Fire. He was playing their hit song "September" at full volume while driving and noticed that his rear-view mirror was vibrating because of the bass. He realized that if he could show the heavy steps of a dinosaur leaving vibrations in a glass of water, he could create a sense of excitement and anticipation for the movie audience. The resulting scene became one of cinema's greatest moments: two children, abandoned in a car, nervously watching water vibrating in two water glasses left on the dashboard with ominous thuds heard in the background.

By looking elsewhere, using Page 2 learning, Spielberg, Nintendo, Compeed and the Bee Gees found unique solutions. Going through a crisis tends to nudge us in new and unexpected directions. We enter a kind of no man's land where rules are upended and we are free to explore the unexplored.

The next chapter will examine why these post-crisis landscapes are excellent springboards for new ideas.

CHAPTER 14
YEAR ZERO

In 1995, a giant bonfire consisting of mobile phones burned in front of Samsung's headquarters. This was not a protest by disgruntled customers; the company itself had set the fire. The phones had been Christmas presents for every employee, but the quality had been so bad that when the complaints started, Samsung's leader, Lee Kun-hee (known as Chairman Lee), took all of them back and decided to burn them. He wanted to set an example – not that complaining was wrong but that the quality of Samsung's products was unacceptable. Chairman Lee gave an impassioned speech in front of the flames and promised to keep burning things if the quality did not improve. This was the beginning of a miraculous journey for the company – from producing cheap electronic gadgets in the 1990s to becoming one of the world's most innovative companies a couple of decades later. There is a saying in Latin: "speramus meliora, resurget cineribus," which means "we hope for better things that will rise from the ashes."

We can discover the new in the smouldering ruins of the old.

What do Ben & Jerry's ice cream and the sports company Nike have in common with the German synth band Kraftwerk and the cryptocurrency Bitcoin? The answer is that they all started in a time of crisis. For Nike and Ben & Jerry's, it was 1970s America with its problems relating to inflation, recession, the ill-advised war in Vietnam, inequality, societal tension and a general feeling that the good years of the 1950s and 1960s were truly over.

For Kraftwerk, it was the fact that German culture had died along with the Nazis. Everything old in Germany was tainted by the supremacist ideology forced upon the people in the 1930s and 1940s. Whereas other artists could build upon a cultural heritage, Kraftwerk could only look to the future.

They explored the recently invented synthesizer and made songs about motorways, fast trains and calculators. When they were celebrated at New York's Museum of Modern Art many years later, the curator would proclaim that the band had anticipated how our lives would change through mobility and technology decades before the iPhone.

Bitcoin was first mentioned in a mysterious essay published in the wake of the 2008 financial crash. Published under the pseudonym Satoshi Nakamoto, it outlined how a decentralized, peer-to-peer digital currency could revolutionize the financial world of banks and money. The old world of big banks had crumbled and something new was being born.

Bitcoin, Kraftwerk, Nike and Ben & Jerry's are testaments to the power of 'Year Zero,' when the old rules and rulers have fallen and we are left to experiment in a void.

Frank Sinatra's most famous and beloved songs came when he was in his forties, after a career slump. Cassius Clay's first boxing career was cut short when he refused to be drafted into the US military. He spent what for others would have been the prime athletic years, the mid-twenties, in exile and unable to practise the sport at which he had excelled. When he returned, he had to develop a new boxing style based on his loss of speed. He had also changed his name. Everything we admire about Muhammad Ali – his wisdom, his legendary bouts – stems from his comeback years, when most athletes would have retired.

The ageing brain is a relatively new academic discipline. One of the most interesting findings so far is how our intelligence changes. It was once believed that it was static – as the crude measurement technique IQ (intelligence quota) can attest. It is now thought that we have two different kinds of intelligence in life.

When we are young, we have fluid intelligence. We are quick-witted and draw conclusions quickly, and our minds can flow through various disciplines quickly.

As we grow older, fluid intelligence subsides and we gain crystallized intelligence. We are not as quick in our judgements and conclusions, but that helps us make better decisions. We can draw upon our experience to express unique ideas.

Artists usually have an early phase, where they are more experimental, and a late style, where they have perfected their craft – fluid versus crystallized creativity.

Literary professor Edward Said described 'late style' as follows: "the artist is no longer under pressure to do other than what they want or need to do, to create out of, the artist's mature subjectivity, stripped of hubris and pomposity, unashamed either of its fallibility or of the modest assurance it has gained as a result of age and exile."

"

The future cannot be predicted, but futures can be invented.

"

Dennis Gabor

When we quote Muhammad Ali – "Don't count the days. Make the days count" – it is late-style Ali, not the speedy youngster Clay, who speaks.

When the old you dies, somebody new is born.

Maybe it is a better you.

CHAPTER 15
DARE TO SUCK

The Welsh designer Ross Lovegrove was tasked with creating a new bottle for the mineral water brand Tŷ Nant, also based in Wales. He doodled on a piece of paper, trying to imitate the flow of water. He then set about sculpting a plastic bottle that would not have the smoothness of other brands but rather be irregularly shaped like a frozen waterfall. It took a long time, and he sighed with disappointment when he saw the finished prototype. He had failed. The bottle looked like nothing and felt like nothing. Then, as he poured water into the bottle, everything changed.

"I realized that I had put a skin on water," Lovegrove would later proclaim. The bottle became an award-winning global phenomenon, making the designer and Tŷ Nant famous. Nothing had become something.

Giving a rating on a linear scale from 1 to 5 has become the standard way to review everything from restaurants and hotel rooms on TripAdvisor to movies and books in newspapers. A rating of 1 means 'really bad' and 5 means 'excellent.' This linear view of quality has a downside for all of us. In our quest to create something worthy of a 5 and out of fear of creating a 1, we usually settle for a 4 or even a strong 3. In our quest to shine, we settle for 'meh.'

This is why we should reframe quality, moving from a 1–5 linear scale to something circular, like a wheel, where the 1 is right next door to the 5 and both are opposite the mediocre middle numbers. It might be called the Wheel of Quality, where you risk a 1 in the hope of achieving a 5.

For something to be the best you have ever done, you need to risk it being the worst you have ever done.

It can be interesting to wander through any modern car park packed with vehicles. Nearly all the cars will be identical. Different brands, yes, but in their overall shapes (and to an extent their colours) they will all be variations on a theme. This was not the case decades ago, when red Cadillac convertibles with wings would stand next to acid green Volkswagen beetles, boxy turquoise Volvos and miniature white Toyotas.

The same is true of mobile phones. They used to come in different shapes, sizes and colours. Even the ringtones varied, from digital beeps to personalized melodies. Today, regardless of brand, you will get a rectangle made of glass and metal.

This is not because companies are dull cowards but because they are savvy. People tend to copy other people. This is known as 'mimetic desire', which says that we do not invent what we desire inside ourselves but rather copy our desires from what we see others want.

This is why a penthouse apartment in the middle of London will be expensive. Many people want to live there. In contrast, a remote farm in Poland will cost you less. Fewer people want to live there.

"

Competent people resist change. Why? Because change threatens to make them less competent. And competent people like being competent. That's who they are; sometimes, that's all they've got. No wonder they're not in a hurry to rock the boat.

"

Seth Godin

FOMO – fear of missing out – exists because we want to do and be where others are.

This is why cars are so homogenous. People will tend to want something sleek, slightly modern-looking and white rather than something angular, yellow and strange-looking.

It is challenging to lead anything remotely different from an ordinary life, but this is why there is tremendous value hidden outside the comfortable path.

And inside the fear of failure.

When Karl Johan Schuster, known as Shellback, was hired as a studio intern for the Swedish music producer Max Martin, he was petrified that his ideas were not good enough. He had a background as a drummer in a grindcore band (a very heavy kind of metal music). Now, he was sitting opposite the American singer Alecia Moore, better known under the moniker P!nk, who was leaning in to hear his ideas for her next song. He was worried that what he was about to play for her was embarrassingly bad. She told him to relax. "Dare to suck," she added, and it became a mantra of sorts for Shellback. As of 2022, he has had over 20 number-one hits worldwide with artists ranging from Kesha to Maroon 5 and Taylor Swift.

When we go through a crisis and fail, the version of us that comes out the other side can be more prone to fear. More eager to fit in. Less keen to take risks. The Wheel of Quality reminds us of the rewards that risk-taking offers.

If we dare to suck.

"

This present moment used to be the unimaginable future.

"

Stewart Brand

PART FOUR

REFRESH
– RESET

CHAPTER 16
THE (OTHER)
BUTTERFLY EFFECT

The robotics start-up iRobot went through 14 failed business models in the early 1990s. The team tried developing a TV shop with robots and tried making robots to handle hazardous waste. They thought licensing robotic technology to the military might work and even tried selling underwater robots. All these attempts failed.

Then they decided to focus their efforts on building a robot vacuum cleaner. It took them two years to get the prototype ready. It looked like something out of a science fiction matinee film with cables and circuits embedded into a giant glass bubble. Aesthetically, it appealed only to junior engineers, primarily boys. If it were to reach a mass market, the team would have to work on the design and ensure that the price came down and the thing worked more reliably. That journey took another ten years. The first Roomba was launched in 2002, a decade after the prototype had been completed. The product struggled to sell in the early years but would become one of the bestselling consumer products within the next decade. It was an overnight success story, 18 years in the making.

But that is nothing if you compare it to the journey of Nespresso. Nestlé filed the patent for selling home-brewed espresso capsules in 1972. It took the company 14 years to get a product out into the market and even then it initially sold only in Japan. It went on to lose money every year until 2006. It is hard to imagine the world without Nespresso shops and George Clooney advertisements today, and it is thanks to Nestlé for not losing faith despite three decades of hardship.

The struggles of iRobot and Nestlé echo Milton's Paradise Lost: "Long is the way and hard, that out of Hell leads up to light."

Failure is where success likes to hide in plain sight. There are countless examples of this. Slack, the near-ubiquitous collaboration tool – began its life as a failed computer game called *Glitch*. Instagram started out as a failed geotagging service called BRBN. Twitter began its life as a failed podcast portal called Odeo. The song "Torn" was recorded by three other artists before it gained worldwide fame with Natalie Imbruglia. Over 40 publishers rejected Douglas Stuart's remarkable novel *Shuggie Bain* before it became a global bestseller. A butterfly does not come into this world as a beautiful winged creature but as a slimy larva. Afterwards it becomes a cocoon, and later a thing of colour and beauty.

Success starts with failure. Trial and error. Experimentation. And our fairy tales of ugly ducklings and frogs being kissed are there to remind us to persevere.

Sir James Black, a Nobel Prize-winning pharmacologist, once said: "It's not a good drug unless it's been killed at least three times." He meant that the path from idea to success is crooked and filled with potholes and pitfalls, just like life.

"

Nothing in a caterpillar tells you it's going to be a butterfly.

"

Buckminster Fuller

It has become fashionable over the past decade to adopt the mindset of Silicon Valley entrepreneurs, where failing is seen as a career path and 'fail fast' is used as a punchy slogan. This contrarian advice is insincere as it is often used by people who have already succeeded. It is easy to talk about the value of failure when you are sitting in a luxury mansion with millions of dollars in the bank. Real-world, real-time failure is a terrifying experience. It can fill you with pain, guilt and shame. Or just a sense of complete emptiness. Most people's gut reaction is to look away from failure, try to avoid it and, when it happens, run away from it.

Clichés like 'embrace failure' are there not to celebrate the f-word but to ask us not to run away from it immediately – to take a second look and understand what happened before we throw the debacle in the trash. The pain will subside eventually.

Time is a healer, but it will only work if we let it. Ignoring things and pushing them down will only make them return unannounced. Joan Didion put it as follows: "I think we are well advised to keep on nodding terms with the people we used to be, whether we find them attractive company or not. Otherwise, they turn up unannounced and surprise us, come hammering on the mind's door at 4 a.m. of a bad night and demand to know who deserted them, who betrayed them, who is going to make amends."

The Californian use of 'failure' described above is a euphemism along the lines of 'veal' instead of 'baby cow' or 'nuggets' instead of 'chopped-up chickens.' It deceives and misleads.

There is a much more helpful – if slightly distasteful – phrase that can be used to describe the humiliation of accepting your errors.

It is 'eating crow.' This slightly repulsive bird is unfit for the human diet, so the basic idea is that eating it – feathers, beak and all – is as difficult as accepting that you have been wrong, that a position you have held turned out to be erroneous and that your mistakes had consequences.

Time is magic. It can transform pain into wisdom and ugly failures into beautiful gems.

CHAPTER 17
THE RESTLESS
BRAIN

Why do so many people go through a mid-life crisis? Why do seemingly successful people self-destruct at the peak of their powers? Why do artists abandon the style or sound that made them famous? And just why did Eve eat the apple, knowing full well that it would get her and her hubby kicked out of paradise?

The answer is that the brain is, above all, restless. It is constantly working to seek new patterns, solutions and possibilities. We humans are also prone to becoming bored, some more easily than others. We are not content to rest on our laurels, no matter how comfortable they are.

This is why crises are often self-made. We had it all, but we wanted to seek out some new state of being where we did not have it, or had something else, or had to fight to get it all back. Until life is over, we are never finished.

Clotaire Rapaille is a French marketing consultant with an unorthodox method. When advising politicians and advertisers on how best to influence voters and consumers, he psychoanalyses people to understand the underlying hopes, fears, and interpretations of culture and society. Over the years, he has pinpointed that most people associate being overweight with 'giving up' and toilet paper with 'freedom' since it enables children to be alone for the first time when they learn to wipe. Rapaille found something exciting when he investigated our relationship with the idea of perfection. Rather than 'perfect' being perceived as positive, he found that the word most commonly associated with it is 'dead.' The dictionary defines 'perfect' as "having all the required or desirable elements, qualities, or characteristics; as good as possible." While this is a worthy aspiration, it is unattainable and fleeting. Like happiness, it can exist for short bursts but not linger for decades.

The Old Testament describes the Garden of Eden as a perfect paradise, a "beautiful garden containing the tree of life, where God intended Adam and Eve to live in peaceful and contented innocence, effortlessly reaping the fruits of the Earth." The key to understanding why exactly anyone would want to break out of this illustrious bubble is that the fruit Eve eats grows on the Tree of Knowledge, and the snake who urges her to break God's taboo promises that it will open her eyes. The Garden of Eden might be pleasant, but it is also stagnant. Outside lie knowledge and insight at the price of sacrificed comfort and convenience. The restlessness of human brains makes us tamper with the things that seem perfect.

This is also why Neo, the main character in *The Matrix* (mentioned in *Chapter 2*), decides to swallow the red pill. He gets a choice between a blue pill – which will leave him enslaved and oblivious, but content in the illusion created by the machines – or a red pill – which will allow him to escape the artificial dream world and enter the much harsher but truthful reality. Neo, like Eve, opts for the latter.

"

A work of art
is never truly
completed, only
abandoned.

"

Paul Valéry

Happiness was once viewed as a binary concept. You were either happy because you embraced religious doctrine or unhappy because you had sinned. With the combination of longer lives, more choices and (in many places) less emphasis on religion as a guiding principle, happiness went from being binary to resembling a mountainous landscape of possibilities. Today, you can explore highs and lows in your pursuit of happiness, from consuming drugs and alcohol (generally speaking, a bad recipe for happiness) to intense physical workouts and reading difficult books (generally speaking, better ideas for happiness). We have been sentenced to freedom, something to which unsolicited advice on social media and self-help books promising 12 ways to find love can attest.

These developments have made restlessness institutionalized. We are expected to explore and not be content with the status quo. Is it any wonder that some people, even most, will make bad choices and hit dead ends in this hedonic maze?

The way to cope with a restless brain is not to switch it off but to find guiding principles that emphasize the long term over the short term. One of the most valuable principles in this context is the importance of incompleteness – of accepting and embracing the fact that things should not be finished. This might suggest a kind of Sagrada Família for the soul – named after the unfinished church in Barcelona that has been under construction, yet magnificent to behold, for over a century.

The economics profession adopted this principle in the 2010s, abandoning the idea of 'economic man', which was the long-held assumption that humans were static in their preferences and rationality. It now sees us in a constant state of 'becoming'. We dream, hope, yearn and are constantly moving towards something. We want to better ourselves, not just stay content.

This creates conflict and friction yet it makes for a more fulfilling life.

An extensive global survey of divorce cases published in the *Journal of Marriage and Family* in 2007 found that more than 60% of divorces happened in so-called low-conflict marriages, where nobody ever raised their voice or argued passionately for something they cared about. This might be comfortable but, judging from the divorce rate, it is unbearable in the long run.

This principle can also be applied on a society-wide level. Orson Welles has a line of dialogue in his masterpiece movie *The Third Man* (1949) outlining why conflict is essential for progress: "In Italy, for 30 years under the Borgias, they had warfare, terror, murder, and bloodshed, but they produced Michelangelo, Leonardo da Vinci, and the Renaissance. In Switzerland, they had brotherly love – they had 500 years of democracy and peace, and what did that produce? The cuckoo clock."

When First Lady Michelle Obama spoke at a college graduation ceremony in 2015, she made the same point. She urged the students to "run towards the noise... to actively seek out the most contentious, polarized, gridlocked places you can find because so often, those have been the places where progress happens."

Society needs its storms.

The brain is restless.

Accept it. Embrace it.

CHAPTER 18
BOUNCEBACKABILITY

Sarah Moore had a dream. And a problem.

She wanted to invest in and own her own company, but she had just graduated from business school and lacked experience, staff and money. She set out to pursue her dream, solving one problem at a time. She began by hiring interns she advertised for on online notice boards and used the school library as her office. The problem was that none of the interns went to the same school as her, so she had to produce fake IDs for them. Together, they ploughed through over 400,000 private companies looking at income, business plans and profitability. To finance the interns' salaries, Moore would participate in medical research studies, although she had to go on an unplanned hiatus when she temporarily lost her vision in a deodorant study.

After a year, she found a company called eggcartons.com, selling, you guessed it, egg cartons.

She wanted to take out a large loan to buy the company and asked banks to help with the financing. The vast majority told her to get lost. Perseverance enabled her to find a bank that would lend. But the current owner of the egg carton business did not want to sell, so she pestered him night and day until he replied, and they agreed on a price.

> **"**
> The idea that the future is unpredictable is undermined every day by the ease with which the past is explained.
> **"**

Daniel Kahneman

She finally made her dream come true.

There are not a lot of Sarah Moores in the world, but most stories about successfully pursuing a dream look like hers – a long string of problems to solve.

Now is probably a good time to admit that the subtitle of this book is misleading. "How to bounce back from a crisis" (a) sounds like it is easy and (b) makes it seem like you will come back to some specific place in time before the crisis happened.

This book has set out to prove that neither is true.

There is no one way to cope after a crisis. It is not about bouncing back; it is about bouncing forward, sideways and even inter-dimensionally. Handling a crisis is not about following a recipe but about developing a skill set called 'bouncebackability.' Moore showed this skill in the story above. She could have given up, blamed the circumstances or felt sorry for herself. Instead, she soldiered on and used adversity as a kind of fuel. She is no superwoman, but her story makes her a hero because we all admire her ability to face adversity with a sense of purpose and grit.

This is why one of the three symbols on the cover of this book is the lotus flower. They rise out of murky water at night and open their unstained blooms to the daylight. In several cultures, they symbolize resilience, strength and rebirth.

When George Lucas was writing *Star Wars Episode IV: A New Hope* – or *Adventures of the Starkiller*, to use his working title – he did not initially have any ideas beyond making a movie with spaceships engaged in a dogfight similar what he'd seen in the war movies he'd loved as a boy. This was hardly enough to make a captivating feature-length narrative.

That was when he remembered his idol, literature professor Joseph Campbell. Campbell is best known for having originated the idea of a hero's journey, wherein somebody who resides in the ordinary world is thrown out into the mysterious unknown because of a chance meeting.

Lucas realized that he would have to craft a fairy tale with relatable characters instead of just showing spaceships flying around the galaxy fighting each other. In the foreground, he placed a farmer's boy who stumbled upon a distress call from a princess. From *Snow White* to *One Thousand and One Nights*, this is one of the most common premise for a narrative. Yet it worked miraculously, and *Star Wars Episode IV* became one of the most successful movies ever made, critically and commercially.

We are all living a hero's journey, but its narrative structure is much messier than what Campbell outlined. Our lives – our futures – are not smooth but jagged.

Imagine if you could travel back to 1938 and somebody asked you what the second half of the 20th century would be like. You would describe all the technological marvels on the horizon, such as aeroplane travel and colour TV. You would show statistics about rising health and longevity, and the fall of poverty and hunger. You would talk about the long peace and prosperity that would reign in Europe and elsewhere.

"However," you might add ominously, "there is something terrible that will happen before all of this can take place – and it is going to happen next year."

This shows how the future can be both good and bad simultaneously. The Second World War was the biggest disaster the modern world had ever encountered and led to killing and suffering on a massive scale. Yet it was followed by some of the most prosperous years the world has ever had.

In turbulent times, bouncebackability is vital. It is an artform, unique and filtered through each and every person's experience of a jagged life.

CHAPTER 19
HOW TO COPE
WITH CRISES

Novelist Emmanuel Carrère was depressed. Worse, he was suicidal. Sitting with his psychotherapist, he shared his inclination to end his life. Instead of contradicting him, the therapist said, "You're right. Suicide doesn't get very good press these days, but sometimes it's the right solution... Or you can live." Carrère listened in stunned silence as the therapist added: "What you're going through is horrible: fine. Live it. Embrace it. Be nothing more than this horror. If you must die, die. Don't look for a reason or a way out. Do nothing, let go: that's the only way things can change."

It is perhaps unsurprising that Carrère shares this anecdote in an autobiographical novel called *Yoga*, since the ancient Indian practice focuses on acceptance and consciousness.

Accepting things exactly as they are is the most challenging thing we are forced to do. This closing chapter will examine some coping mechanisms we can use to help us in this quest.

A crisis happens when expectations and reality collide. You cannot control reality, but you can manage your expectations. One rule of thumb you might consider adopting is that expectations are almost always distorted. We expect bad things to be worse than they are and good things to be better. We tend to misjudge risks and assume that spectacular, rare things will happen to us, and at the same time we believe we are somehow immune to common hazards such as having a fall or a high cholesterol level.

The key is not to build some meticulously crafted but quickly outdated model of the specific risks and rewards that you face. Prospective risk management exercises are fine for bureaucratic organizations but cumbersome for individuals. The key is to accept your broken expectations and adjust them downwards. As *Chapter 15, Dare to Suck*, explored, it is rare to lead a life outside the ordinary, and the trials and tribulations you face will resemble those others have encountered. The beauty of this insight is that there is bound to be a book, a blog entry or an article written about the same thing you are going through right now. You may feel lost and isolated in your pain, shame or guilt, but you are never alone.

In the movie *The Truman Show*, the main character is, unbeknownst to him, part of an elaborate 24-hour reality soap opera. His wife, his best friend, and all the staff and residents filling up the tiny seaside town where the show is set are hired actors. The movie has given rise to a psychological delusion called Truman Show Delusion. It arises when people believe they are being watched 24/7 and are part of the same elaborate, sinister kind of televised entertainment.

Most people suffer from a light version of this delusion because they place too much emphasis on themselves. Individualism has, in general, brought many good things into our lives. We have more freedom to choose what to do, whom we will be and with whom we will spend our lives. The downside is that we place ourselves at the centre of life. This is fine as long as we accept that everybody else is doing the same thing. Nobody is as invested in your problems as you, and nobody cares as much about your failures and shortcomings. That thing that happened last year or ten years ago that you are still mentally regurgitating – nobody else in the world is thinking about it. Everybody is busy thinking about themselves and coping with life.

This is a source of consolation, not isolation.

When the writer Oliver Burkeman wrote his last column for *The Guardian* in 2020, he summarized what he had learned over the years writing life-changing advice. One point is particularly relevant to this book: the future will never provide the reassurance you seek from it. Misery arises from trying to control what we cannot. The future – a blank canvas for dreams and nightmares – will forever be uncertain, contested and contestable. Believing in prophecy will only cause misery. Hoarding money to control your destiny will make enjoying the moment more challenging. The future is promised to no one. If you plan to wait for someone to come and save you, you need a better plan. No one is coming. Your life is your responsibility.

If you were to swim long enough in cream, it would become sufficiently solid for you to climb out of the bowl. That is the magic of time and persistence.

A crisis distorts our sense of time. All of a sudden, days rush by or take forever. We feel pressure to do things more quickly, increasing our risk of failure. We overestimate what we can get done in a year and underestimate what we can get done in a decade. One of the most critical things in coping with a crisis is your view of time. Assume that you have more of it. Slow it down. Add another decade. Remember what the Russian author Leo Tolstoy said: "time and patience are the strongest warriors."

This too shall pass.

"

Wait. Ten seconds. Ten years. The world figures out what it wants to do.

"

Susan Straight

CONCLUSION:
KINTSUGI

The most durable materials in the world are soft, not hard. Aeroplanes land on tyres made of rubber, not titanium. Graphene – a flexible, bendable carbon composite material – is ten times stronger than steel. And an idea, in and of itself weightless and invisible, can last for millennia, whereas most buildings and structures are gone within a century or two.

Humans are soft but we harden, believing that strength is based on solidity and robustness. Even our metaphors mislead us into a state of stasis. We seek 'balance' and believe it to be a place of calm in a storm. However, if you watch someone balancing on a tightrope, you see that balance is completely different. Far from staying still, the balancing act is made possible through small, rapid, constant movements to adjust for microscopic movements in the rope and the surroundings.

Stability is created by constant movement.

Life will never be the same again. That is the underlying, slightly unnerving, message in every crisis.

In the space of a few years, I lost my business, my marriage and my sense of self-worth. My life, as I had once known it, was broken.

> # For all that has been, Thank you. For all that is to come, Yes!

Dag Hammarskjöld

But not beyond repair.

In the aftermath, I gained wisdom and changed my business. My wife and I recalibrated our relationship and remarried in an Elvis chapel in Las Vegas.

Slowly, a new kind of self-worth emerged. Not the adolescent sense of omnipotence that I'd had in my thirties but one based on humility and openness. A more comforting kind of self-worth.

This book has attempted to outline the phases of a crisis and how we can best prepare for and cope with the things that happen to us, for us and with us in life. If I were to summarize it in one word, I would use the Japanese *kintsugi*. This is an art form wherein you seek to repair broken pottery by filling the cracks with precious metal, such as gold or silver. Instead of disguising the cracks, you elevate them into something beautiful. As a philosophy, *kintsugi* treats breakage and repair as part of the history of an object.

Take the experiences of life over the perfection of life.

You will lose your way and find it again.

And again.

REFERENCES

INTRODUCTION

Sources/References

The epigraph is from L'Amour, Louis. *Lonely on the Mountain: A Novel (Sacketts)*. Fifth or Later Edition. Bantam, 1984.

"Everybody loves a winner, but when you lose, you lose alone" is a song by William Bell, 1967

THE GROUNDHOG WAY

The epigraph is from Kafka, Franz. *Letters to Friends, Family and Editors*. Schocken, 1990.

Second epigraph from deGrasse Tyson, Neil. Starry Messenger: *Cosmic Perspectives on Civilization*: Chapter 2: Exploration & Discovery. 2022, Henry Holt and Co.

Danny Rubin and Harold Ramis using Elisabeth Kübler-Ross' model is from Gilbey, Ryan. Groundhog Day. London: British Film Institute, 2004. Page 49.

The tweet by WHO is still up:
https://twitter.com/who/status/1217043229427761152?lang=en

CHAPTER 1: DELIGHTFUL DELUSIONS

The epigraph is from Herman, Judith Lewis. *Trauma and Recovery: The Aftermath of Violence*. Basic Books, 1997. Page 38.

The quote and story about Tower Records is from Hanks, C. (Director). (2015). All Things Must Pass: The Rise and Fall of Tower Records [Film].

Norman Angell's book is
Angell, Norman. *The Great Illusion: A Study of the Relation of Military Power to National Advantage*. CreateSpace Independent Publishing Platform, 2018.

The selected quote of Angell is from
Joll, James. *The Origins of the First World War*. Longman, 1992. p.202

The list of biases is taken from Wikipedia. Lost of Cognitive Biases, (accessed on 2022-08-01)

CHAPTER 2: OSTRICH MODE

The epigraph is from Shakespeare, William. *Cymbeline*. Modern Library, 2011. Act 4, Scene 2.

The Hero's Journey is a concept coined and described by Campbell, Joseph. *The Hero with a Thousand Faces*. 21st edition. Princeton: Princeton University Press, 1973.

The lyrics are taken from *Titanic (Andraklasspassagerarens sista sång).* Song by Mikael Wiehe, 1978. Used with generous permission from United Stage Publishing AB

Steve Ballmer's quote is from The Times of India (2022) Watch: When Microsoft CEO Steve Ballmer laughed at iPhone.
(Accessed: 3 August, 2022)

The examples of failed businesses – Laura Ashley, Kodak and Volkswagen – taken from Sull, Donald N. *Why Good Companies Go Bad And How Great Managers Remake Them*. Revised Edition. Cambridge: Harvard University Press, 2005.

CHAPTER 3: SUCCESS IS TOXIC

Epigraph taken from
Bronson, Po. *What Should I Do with My Life?* 1st Edition. Random House Trade Paperbacks, 2003.

The story of Nokia's chairman Risto Siilasmaa taken from
Siilasmaa, Risto. *Transforming NOKIA: The Power of Paranoid Optimism to Lead Through Colossal Change*. 1st Edition. McGraw Hill, 2018.

Francis Fukuyama's article is
Fukuyama, Francis. "The End of History?" *Center for the National Interest* No. 16 (Summer 1989), pp. 3-18. https://www.jstor.org/stable/24027184

The book is Fukuyama, Francis. *The End of History and the Last Man*. Free Press, 1992.

The story of George Michael taken from
Gavin, James. *George Michael: A Life*. Harry N. Abrams, 2022.

CHAPTER 4: KANSAS MOMENTS
Epigraph taken from
Herbert, Frank. *God Emperor of Dune*. Ace, 2019.

The story of Kathryn Schulz is taken from
Schulz, Kathryn. *Lost & Found: Reflections on Grief, Gratitude, and Happiness*. Random House Trade Paperbacks, 2022.

Joan Didion's book is
Didion, Joan. *The Year of Magical Thinking*. 1st Edition. Alfred A. Knopf, 2005.

The study from Turin about The Wizard of Oz is
Bioglio, L. & Pensa, R. G. (2018). *Identification of key films and personalities in the history of cinema from a Western perspective, Applied Network Science, Volume 3, Article number: 50*
https://appliednetsci.springeropen.com/articles/10.1007/s41109-018-0105-0

The happiness research referenced is from Gilbert, Daniel. *Stumbling on Happiness*. 1st Edition, Alfred A. Knopf, 2006.

CHAPTER 5: THE GROUCHO MARX PRINCIPLE

The epigraph is from
Jung, C.G. Modern Man in Search of a Soul. Martino Fine Books, 2011.

The story of Stig and the tsunami taken from
"Sommar i P1: Pigge Werkelin" Sveriges Radio, August 7, 2005. Sweden.
https://sverigesradio.se/avsnitt/359923

The quote from Groucho Marx is from
Simple, J. (2016) *Groucho Marx's Comedy Is Pure, Bleak Nihilism, slate.com*
https://slate.com/culture/2016/01/groucho-marx-the-comedy-of-existence-by-lee-siegel-reviewed.html

Esther Perel's research is taken from
Perel, Esther. *The State of Affairs: Rethinking Infidelity*. Harper, 2017.
The direct quote is from page 98.

CHAPTER 6 BREAKING THE LOOP OF DENIAL

The epigraph is from
Orwell, George. *The Collected Essays, Journalism, and Letters of George Orwell*. 1st Edition, David R. Godine, 2002.

The second epigraph is from a tweet by Trent Shelton, May 8, 2020

The Thomas Wolsey quote is from
Irish, Bradley J. *Emotion in the Tudor Court: Literature, History, and Early Modern Feeling*. Northwestern University Press, 2018.

The ancient myth about the king and his son is told in
Taleb, Nicholas Nassim. *Antifragile: Things That Gain from Disorder*. First Edition,
Random House, 2012.

CHAPTER 7: WHY DOES IT ALWAYS RAIN CHEESE ON ME?

The title is close to title of a Travis song, *Why Does It Always Rain On Me?* Written by
Fran Healy. Published by Independiente, 1999.

The epigraph is from
De La Cruz, Melissa. The Isle of the Lost. Disney-Hyperion, 2015.

Sophie Freud's insight is quoted in
Robert, S. (2022) *Sophie Freud, Critic of Her Grandfather's Gospel, Dies at 97*. New York
Times. https://www.nytimes.com/2022/06/03/science/sophie-freud-dead.html

The Swiss Cheese model is taken from
Anon. (n.d.), Swiss cheese model, Wikipedia, Retrieved November 8 2022
https://en.wikipedia.org/wiki/Swiss_cheese_model

Thoughts on the human fascination with competitive sports taken from
Norberg, Johan. *Open: The Story of Human Progress*. Atlantic Books, 2020.

CHAPTER 8: A SIMPLE RECIPE FOR DEFUSING EMOTIONS AND HARVESTING LUCK

The epigraph is from
"Jim Carrey at MIU: Commencement Address at the 2014 Graduation." YouTube, uploaded by
Maharishi International University, 30 May 2014, www.youtube.com/watch?v=V80-gPkpH6M.

The story of Olle is described in the song *Trubbel*, written by Olle Adolphson, Published by
Telefunken, 1961.

The history of John Walker is taken from
Anon. (n.d.), Johnnie Walker, Wikipedia, retrieved November 8 2022
https://en.wikipedia.org/wiki/Johnnie_Walker

The quote on going through hell is taken from Christian Science Monitor and described at
https://quoteinvestigator.com/2014/09/14/keep-going/
Retrieved on November 21, 2022.

The research into alcohol and driving comes from
Alcohol Alters Prefrontal Cortex Activity Through Ion Channel Disruption, Alcoholism:
Clinical & Experimental Research, April 3, 2008
https://www.sciencedaily.com/releases/2008/04/080403183048.htm

The research on luck and success is from
Kaufman, Scott B. (2018) *The Role of Luck in Life Success Is Far Greater Than We Realized*. Scientific American, https://blogs.scientificamerican.com/beautiful-minds/the-role-of-luck-in-life-success-is-far-greater-than-we-realized/

The story of Mohammed Zahir Shah's assassination attempt taken from
Bergen, Peter. *The Rise and Fall of Osama bin Laden*, First Edition, Simon & Schuster, 2021.

The story of Dire Straits comes from
https://forums.stevehoffman.tv/threads/recording-dire-straits-money-for-nothing.8938/
Retrieved on August 1, 2022.

The story of Jennifer Doudna and Emmanuelle Charpentier comes from
Krämer, K (2020) *How Crispr went from niche to Nobel*. Chemistry World,
https://www.chemistryworld.com/features/how-crispr-went-from-niche-to-nobel/4012604.article

The input/output effect is described at
https://www.theschooloflife.com/article/the-outputinput-confusion/?/

The story of Andrew Lloyd Webber and Starlight Express is taken from
Anon. (n.d.), Starlight Express, Wikipedia, retrieved November 8 2022 https://en.wikipedia.org/wiki/Starlight_Express

CHAPTER 9: LONG LIVE SUFFERING!

The epigraph is from
Barnes, Julian. *Levels of Life*. Random House, 2014.

The research about happiness at Stanford is
Baumeister, Roy F., Vohs, Kathleen D., Aaker, Jennifer & Garbinsky Emily N. (2013) *Some Key Differences between a Happy Life and a Meaningful Life*. Journal of Positive Psychology 2013 Vol. 8 Issue 6

The Seneca quote is from
Seneca the Younger, Hercules Furens, 656.

Rachel Cusk's quote is from
Cusk, Rachel. *Aftermath: On Marriage and Separation*. Reprint Edition, Picador, 2013.

The study of group dynamics is taken from
Anon. (n.d.), Tuckman's stages of group development, Wikipedia, retrieved August 8 2022
https://en.wikipedia.org/wiki/Tuckman's_stages_of_group_development

Chris Martin's quote is from
Johnston, K. (2021) London Grammar's Hannah Reid learnt two big lessons from Chris Martin. GQ Magazine. https://www.gq-magazine.co.uk/gq-hype/article/hannah-reid-london-grammar-interview

The quote about Hilary Mantel is from
Shulevitz, J. (2022) *Hilary Mantel's art was infused with her pain.* The Atlantic. https://www.theatlantic.com/books/archive/2022/09/hilary-mantel-dies-wolf-hall-legacy/671554/

Uphill Decisions is a concept coined by Tim Denning.
https://timdenning.com/heres-how-to-make-the-decisions-that-can-finally-change-your-life-in-a-year/

CHAPTER 10: THE SECOND MOUNTAIN

The epigraph is from
Alighieri, Dante. *The Divine Comedy: Inferno, Purgatorio, Paradiso.* Royal Classics, 2021.

The Second Mountain concept and quote is from
Brooks, David. *The Second Mountain: The Quest for a Moral Life.* First Edition, Random House, 2019.
The quote is taken from page 31.

Hirohito's surrender broadcast is taken from
Anon. (n.d.), Hirohito Surrender Broadcast, Wikipedia, retrieved June 22 2022
https://en.wikipedia.org/wiki/Hirohito_surrender_broadcast

The story of Shinkansen is taken from
Nishiyama, Takashi. (2015). Engineering War and Peace in Modern Japan, 1868-1964. The Journal of Japanese Studies. Vol. 41, No. 2.
https://www.jstor.org/stable/43917714

The story about Mike Posner is from
Impaulsive. Mike Posner Explains Why He Took A Pill In Ibiza [Video]. YouTube.
https://www.youtube.com/watch?v=K-XckKrNDv0

The story of Ole Kirk Christiansen and LEGO is from
Anon. (n.d.), Ole Kirk Christiansen, Wikipedia, retrieved September 1 2022
https://en.wikipedia.org/wiki/Ole_Kirk_Christiansen

CHAPTER 11: THE ALIEN WAY

The epigraph and the story of Petrarch finding the documents is from
Wright, L. (2020) How Pandemics Wreak Havoc and Open Minds. New Yorker.
https://www.newyorker.com/magazine/2020/07/20/
how-pandemics-wreak-havoc-and-open-minds

The story of how the Renaissance changed society is from
The Renaissance Afterlife of Boethius's Moral Allegory of Fortuna. Chapter. In Fortune's
Theatre. Cambridge University Press, 2021.

Otto Von Bismarck's quote is from
Pflanze, Otto (1958). *Bismarck's "Realpolitik". The Review of Politics
Vol. 20, No. 4.*

The comment about AlphaGo was made by
Knight, W. (2017) *Alpha Zero's "Alien" Chess Shows the Power, and the Peculiarity, of AI.*
MIT Technology Review.
https://www.technologyreview.com/2017/12/08/147199/
alpha-zeros-alien-chess-shows-the-power-and-the-peculiarity-of-ai/

The story of John Naissbit is from
Risen, C. (2021). *John Naisbitt, Business Guru and Author of 'Megatrends,' Dies at 92.*
New York Times. https://www.nytimes.com/2021/04/14/books/john-naisbitt-dead.html

CHAPTER 12: FEED THE WELL

Epigraph is taken from
Attention and Creative Imagination in the Work of Simone Weil and János Pilinszky, Chapter in
The Arts of Attention, L'Harmattan, 2016.

The story and quotes about Tom Petty are taken from
Rubin, R. (Host). (2020, October 15). *Tom Petty's "Wildflowers" II with Adria Petty* in
Broken Record. Pushkin Industries. https://www.pushkin.fm/podcasts/broken-record/
tom-pettys-wildflowers-ii-with-adria-petty

The history of the internet and ARPANET from
Anon. (n.d.), ARPANET, Wikipedia, retrieved September 1 2022
https://en.wikipedia.org/wiki/ARPANET

Martijn Verbove's insight is taken from
Verbove, M. (2022). The Metasphere. Martijn Verbove Webscape. https://verbove.com/
twitter/the-metasphere

CHAPTER 13: LOOK ELSEWHERE

The epigraph is from
Ridley, Matt. *The Rational Optimist: How Prosperity Evolves*. Harper, 2010.

Sahil Bloom described Page 2 learning in his Twitter-feed
https://twitter.com/sahilbloom/status/1530548126091726848

The story about the Bee Gees is from
Marshall, F. (Director). (2020). The Bee Gees: How Can You Mend a Broken Heart [Film].

Exaptation is a term described in
Gould, S. J., & Vrba, E. (1982). Exaptation-A Missing Term in the Science of Form.
Paleobiology. https://doi.org/10.1017/S0094837300004310

Compeed is described in a personal interview with Lars Backsell, previously described in
Lindkvist, Magnus. *The Attack of The Unexpected*. Marshall Cavendish, 2010.

Nintendo Wii is described in
Michel, M. (2006, December 21). At the Heart of the Wii, Micron-Size Machines.
New York Times.

The story about Jurassic Park is described in
Kemp, S. (2022, August 28). How Earth Wind & Fire influenced Steven Spielberg movie
'Jurassic Park'. Far Out Magazine.

CHAPTER 14: YEAR ZERO

The epigraph is from
Gabor, Dennis. *Inventing the future*. Knopf, 1971.

The story about Samsung's bonfire is from
Sullivan, M. (2016, October 14). Samsung's Chairman Lee ordered a bonfire of defective
phones in 1995. *Fast Company*.

The story about Kraftwerk is from
Gradvall, J. (2020, May 10). Därför blev Kraftwerk det största bandet efter Beatles. Expressen.

The quote about the MOMA exhibitions is from
https://www.moma.org/calendar/exhibitions/1240
Retrieved on November 21, 2022.

Crystallized vs Fluid intelligence is taken from
(2021). How We Use Fluid vs. Crystallized Intelligence. PsychCentral.
https://psychcentral.com/health/fluid-vs-crystallized-intelligence#crystallized-intelligence

Edward Said's thoughts and quote on late style is from
Said, E. (2004, August 5). Thoughts on Late Style. London Review of Books.

Muhammed Ali's quote is from
(2016). Muhammad Ali's 10 best quotes. ESPN.
https://www.espn.com/boxing/story/_/id/15930888/muhammad-ali-10-best-quotes

CHAPTER 15: DARE TO SUCK

The epigraph is from
Godin, S. (1999, December 31). Change Agent. *Fast Company*.

The second epigraph is from an artwork by Alicia Eggert using a quote by futurist Steward
Brand.

The story about Ross Lovegrove and quote is from
TED. (2007, January 16). Ross Lovegrove: The power and beauty of organic design [Video].
YouTube. https://www.youtube.com/watch?v=sWqkKYwvTNw

The story about Pink and Shellback is from
(2017). Shellback Twitter Entry. Twitter. https://twitter.com/shellback666/
status/918890631807737856?lang=en

CHAPTER 16: THE (OTHER) BUTTERFLY EFFECT

The epigraph is from
Leyla, A. (2016, June 10). Six Powerful insights from the creative shape shifter, R.
Buckminster Fuller. Medium.

The history of the Roomba is taken from
iRobot: From Bomb Squads to Roombas, Here's What This Company Does. History-
Computer, May 7 2022.
https://bityl.co/H2Yx

The history of Nespresso taken from
Anon. (n.d.), Nespresso, Wikipedia, Retrieved August 8 2022
https://en.wikipedia.org/wiki/Nespresso

The Paradise Lost quote is from
Milton, John. *Paradise Lost*. Digireads.com, 2016.

The myriad examples from Odeo, Glitch, Shuggie Bain, etc are gathered and described in
Gradvall, Jan., & Lindkvist, Magnus. *Kreativ Friktion*. Volante, 2021.

The Sir James Black quote is from
Bahcall, Sahil. *Loonshots: How to Nurture the Crazy Ideas That Win Wars, Cure Diseases, and Transform Industries*. St. Martin's Press, 2019.

The Joan Didion quote is taken from
Didion, Joan. *Slouching Towards Bethlehem: Essays*. Reprint Edition. Picador, 2017.

CHAPTER 17: THE RESTLESS BRAIN

The epigraph is from
Valéry, P. (1933, March 1). Le Cimetière marin. La Nouvelle Revue Française.

The examples about Clotaire Rapaille are taken from
Rapaille, Clotaire. *The Culture Code: An Ingenious Way to Understand Why People Around the World Live and Buy as They Do*. Crown Business, 2006.

This definition of "perfect" is from
https://www.encyclopedia.com/literature-and-arts/language-linguistics-and-literary-terms/language-and-linguistics/perfect

The evolution of the economics profession is taken from
Roberts, Russ. *Wild Problems: A Guide to the Decisions That Define Us*. Portfolio, 2022.

The Journal of Marriage and Family article referenced is from
Amato, Paul, and Hohmann-Marriott, Bryndl. "A Comparison of High- and Low-Distress Marriages That End in Divorce." Journal of Marriage and Family, 2007, https://doi.org/https://www.jstor.org/stable/4622471.

The quote by Michelle Obama is from
Bailey, Alyssa. "Michelle Obama to College Graduates: "Run Toward the Noise"."
Elle, 26 May 2015.

CHAPTER 18: BOUNCEBACKABILITY

The epigraph is taken from
Kahneman, Daniel. *Thinking Fast and Slow*. First Edition. Farrar, Straus and Giroux, 2011.

The story about Sarah Moore is from Shaan Puri on Twitter. Thread:
https://twitter.com/shaanvp/status/1552758018797842432

The story about George Lucas and Joseph Campbell is taken from
Baxter, John. *George Lucas: A Biography*. Harper Collins Entertainment, 1999.

CHAPTER 19: HOW TO COPE WITH CRISES

The epigraph is taken from
Straight, Susan. *Mecca*. Farrar, Straus and Giroux, 2022.

The story of Emmanuel Carrère's depression is taken from
Carrère, Emmanuel. *Yoga*. Farrar, Straus and Giroux, 2022.

Oliver Burkeman's last column is
Burkeman, Oliver. "Oliver Burkeman's last column: the eight secrets to a (fairly) fulfilled life." The Guardian, 4 Sept. 2020.

Leo Tolstoy's quote is from
Tolstoy, Leo. *War and Peace*. Arcturus Publishing Limited, 2019.

CONCLUSION: KINTSUGI

The epigraph is taken from
Hammarskjöld Dag. Markings. Ballantine Books, 1985.

ABOUT THE AUTHOR

MAGNUS LINDKVIST is a trendspotter and futurologist. He calls his work "intellectual acupuncture" aiming to change how we think about the future by provoking us with ideas, enabling new questions and challenging our world view. He lives in Stockholm, Sweden together with his wife Vesna and two children.

Contact the author for advice, training, or speaking opportunities: **www.magnuslindkvist.com**

Also by the author:
Everything We Know Is Wrong, 2009
The Attack of The Unexpected, 2010
When The Future Begins, 2013
The Minifesto, 2016
The Future Book, 2023

BY THE SAME AUTHOR

£9.99/$12.95
ISBN: 978-1-911687-87-0